THE HIERARCHY OF HUMOR

GRANT SNIDER

BY MICHAEL GERBER

HELLO, MR. PRESIDENT...

Donald, dude — wanna be adored? Wanna crush your enemies? Resign NOW.

Hello?

...

Yeah, right. The only people up this late are foreigners and college kids.

...

And you, yes. You do sound like him.

...

Hell, no! And Soros didn't pay me a dime.

...

OK, fine: "*President* Trump."

...

"*Mister* President Trump." Donald, it's late. I have a busy day tomorrow. Why are you bothering me?

...

Because we share a birthday. Ladies and gentlemen, the mind that brought you the border wall.

...

Oh, no, I think it's a *great* idea. Walls always work. Thanks to the Great Wall, China's had the same emperor for 2,000 years. And Hadrian's Wall? The only reason the Romans are still ruling Scotland. The Berlin Wall worked so well, they pulled it down in '89 after the whole world went Communist.

...

Yes, I'm joking.

...

Well, "your base" are fools. And the rest of the country wouldn't piss on you if you were on fire.

...

No, not even if you paid them... Could you turn the TV down? By the way, those copper bracelets are a scam.

...

Donald, that makes no sense. You're massively unpopular, deal with it. It's like the election: If the Democrats had rigged it, you would've lost. If the media were cooking the polls, you'd be at, I don't know, 4% or something.

...

We'll just have to agree to disagree then. *I* think you make people think of nuclear war and rape.

...

You call me at 1 AM, crunching Doritos into my ear, and *I'm* rude?

...

I haven't, but I'm sure Dinty Moore out of the can won't kill you. The FDA would shut 'em down.

...

If I tell you what it stands for, you'll dismantle it. Eat the stew or don't. Is that it? Can I go?

...

So why did you run in the first place?

...

Uh huh. I think you didn't expect to win, won, realized you were screwed, and decided to pull a Tom Sawyer.

...

Get other people to do the work, while you chill at Mar-a-Lago making sure there's fresh Viagra in every nightstand.

...

Awful. Just the worst ever. But I think you could be a great *ex*-president.

...

That's exactly what I'm saying. You're 70, man. Who needs it? Every day, the country will just hate you more.

...

Because, democracy. We the people elect someone to blame for everything.

...

Resigning's the only way you *can* win. Declare victory, walk away. Say you're doing it "for the good of the country." *Lie.*

...

Basic math, your approval rating would go from 35% to 65% overnight. Yes, if you resign, Steve Bannon might turn into the Joker, but that's a risk I think we all should take.

...

Bannon looks awful. I think he's Patient Zero for some disease we haven't discovered yet.

...

What it's "supposed to mean" is: Are Bannon's insides liquefying? Call the CDC stat.

...

I'm not going to tell you what it stands for. You'll hand it to some rich goof who believes in "the power of prayer."

...

Fine, don't believe me. Just don't let Bannon lick you. You already look tired.

...

Oh c'mon. Next to Bannon, we all shine like Christ. And Miller— he looks like a 14-year-old who was kicked out of the Science Fair because his project was about eugenics.

...

Racial stuff. Donald, Mr. Cirrhosis and Mr. Psychosis are not your "wingmen"! They are losers.

...

Right. Now expand that loyalty to the entire country, and that's how to be President... What's that sound?

...

I didn't know there was "a Nixon ice machine." I wouldn't eat ice from that. I bet Nixon booby-trapped a whole bunch of stuff on his way out. You could do that. Hide porn with Pence's name on it.

...

Are you nuts? The media would cry bitter tears if you left. *WaPo* just added 60 reporters. Wanna screw them? Resign.

...

Your base would get over it. They could spend the rest of their lives feeling like victims, which is all they really want.

...

Yeah, I guess it is a little like negging. And not that you care, but liberals would become your biggest fans. We love to forgive. It makes us feel superior, which is so much better than winning.

...

Are you kidding me? She'd eat her own liver. *You* got the job she always wanted,

MICHAEL GERBER (@mgerber937) is Editor & Publisher of *The American Bystander*.

and then walked away. Total alpha move.

…

So replace Pence with Ta-Nehisi Coates.

…

To screw Ryan and McConnell, obviously. Donald, why do you think they've let you keep your businesses? So the moment you do something they don't like, they can impeach you.

…

Get real, dude. As long as you're president, *Ryan and McConnell own you*. And you'll get blamed for all their shitty obsessions as well as yours. Donald, these new friends of yours suck. We both know that you'd be a lot more popular if Howard Stern was your chief of staff.

…

You don't think you're getting bad advice? Since when do you, a man who knows the value of a fine Russian prostitute, give a shit about public broadcasting? Donald J. Trump cares about two things: stuff that gets him laid, and stuff that gets him paid. I'm not judging. It's why you

were so popular on TV.

…

Being president isn't like being on TV — who told you it would be like that?

…

Oh, that guy. What's he got on you? Actually don't tell me—

…

LA LA LA NOT LISTENING LA LA —

…

Shit, you did *that*? Is this line secure?

…

I think that just means your Wi-Fi is on.

…

OK, listen: The day you resign, release it yourself, and say Vlad is "kink-shaming" you. Then go on Dan Savage's podcast.

…

I know *exactly* what life would be like: Think Rodney Dangerfield in *Back to School*, but with Secret Service protection.

…

It's pure you: all the media coverage, but none of the responsibility. One week after you walk away, show up at a frat party

at Auburn and do some kegstands. The whole South would *shit*. Go to Hawaii and release video of you trying to do the limbo. Eat a Pink's hot dog with Ron Jeremy. You think you have Twitter followers now? Jesus Christ, you'd break the internet.

…

Yes, well, I think it's a little late to worry about the dignity of the office.

…

Because I think you're going to keel over, man. There's only one way for a guy like you to go out, and that's huffing and puffing over some bored young lady with a cheap French manicure. Not at some stupid day job.

…

Damn it, I'm begging you: *walk away*. It's the right thing for everybody. Except Bannon. Seriously: Don't let him lick you.

…

Well, I've never done that but Donald, if you resign, I will totally ride Jetskis with you. On *our* birthday. Good night. **B**

TABLE OF CONTENTS

DEBRA L. ROTHENBERG

Just one of the NYC bars you must visit before you die next Tuesday.
See the others on Page 54.

The AMERICAN BYSTANDER

Vol. 1, No. 4 • Spring-ish 2017

EDITOR & PUBLISHER
Michael Gerber
HEAD WRITER Brian McConnachie
SENIOR EDITOR Alan Goldberg
DEPUTY EDITORS
Michael Thornton, Ben Orlin

CONTRIBUTORS
Ron Barrett, Charles Barsotti, Louisa Bertman, Adrian Bonenberger, Chris Bonno, George Booth, Andy Breckman, Steve Brodner, Dylan Brody, M.K. Brown, Mark Bryan, Roz Chast, David Chelsea, Howard Cruse, John Cuneo, Etienne Delessert, Nick Downes, Larry Doyle, Liana Finck, James Folta, Treasure Frey, Drew Friedman, Daniel Galef, Tom Gammill, James Finn Gardner, Rick Geary, Django Gold, Alan Goldberg, Geoffrey Golden, Joey Green, Sam Gross, Bob Grossman, Broti Gupta, Jack Handey, Todd Hanson, Quentin Hardy, Tim Harrod, Sam Henderson, J. Jonik, Ted Jouflas, Farley Katz, Joe Keohane, Doug Kirby, Adam Koford, Arnie Kogen, Jay Kogen, Paul Krassner, Ken Krimstein, Peter Kuper, Rob Kutner, Paul Lander, M. Sweeney Lawless, Kit Lively, Merrill Markoe, Scott Marshall, Matt Matera, P.S. Mueller, Joe Oesterle, Ben Orlin, Dennis Perrin, Ethan Persoff, Jonathan Plotkin, Mimi Pond, Mike Reddy, Debra L. Rothenberg, Jay Ruttenberg, Mike Sacks, Cris Shapan, Mike Shear, Mike Shiell, Michael Sloan, Grant Snider, Rich Sparks, Nick Spooner, B.K. Taylor, Steve Torelli, Joe Veix, Armando Veve, Evan Waite, D. Watson, J.A. Weinstein, Andrew Weldon, Shannon Wheeler, Mike Wilkins, Steve Young, Jack Ziegler, Alan Zweibel.
COPYEDITING
Cheryl Levenbrown, God bless 'er
THANKS TO
Kate Powers, Rae Barsotti, Lanky Bareikis, Jon Schwarz, Alleen Schultz, Molly Bernstein, Joe Lopez, Eliot Ivanhoe, Neil Gumenick, Thomas Simon, Elise Brisco, Cathy Spaulding and many, many others.
NAMEPLATES BY
Mark Simonson
ISSUE CREATED BY
Michael Gerber

BOOTH

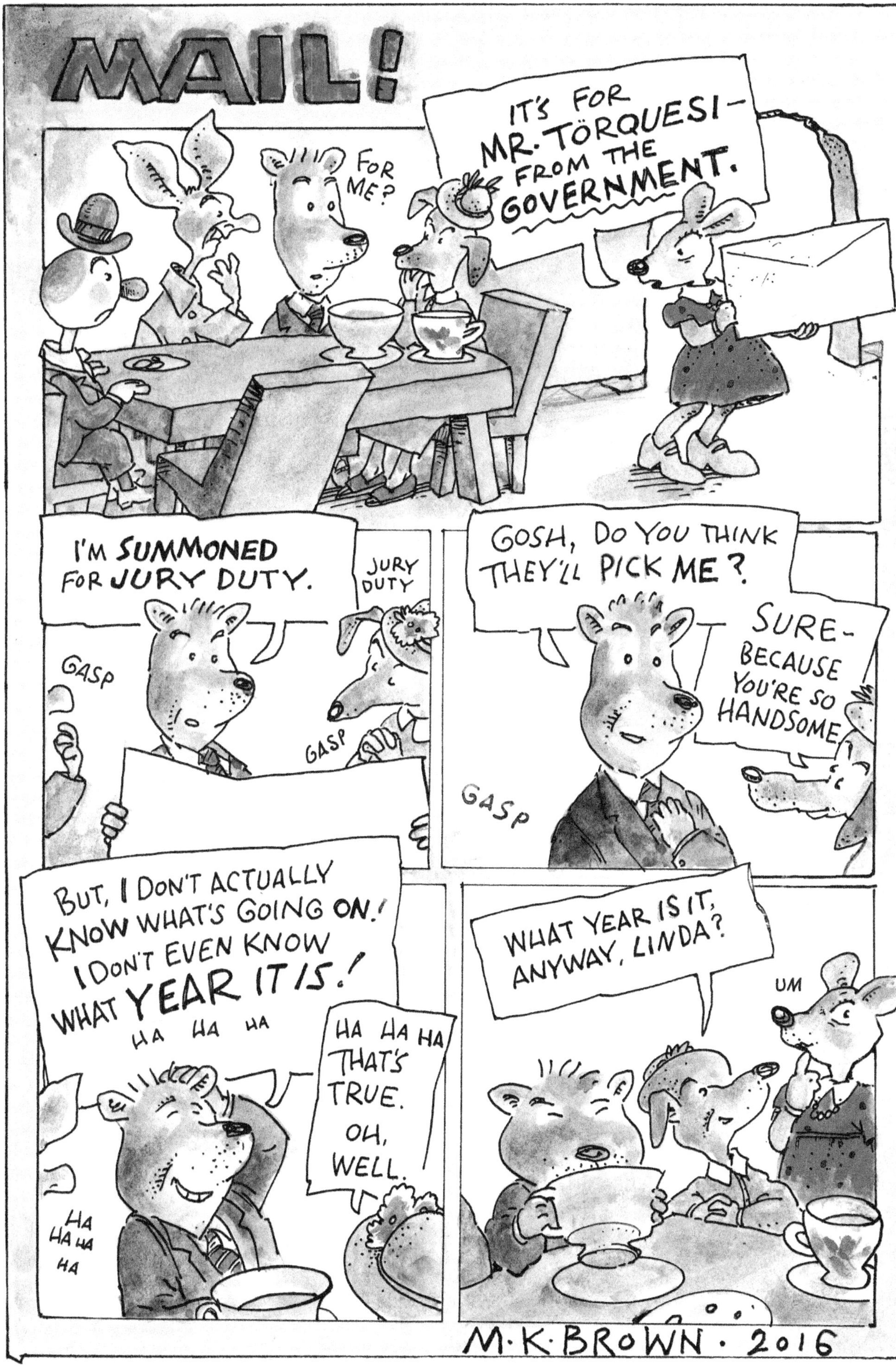
MAIL!
FOR ME?
IT'S FOR MR. TÖRQUESI— FROM THE GOVERNMENT.
I'M SUMMONED FOR JURY DUTY.
JURY DUTY
GASP
GASP
GOSH, DO YOU THINK THEY'LL PICK ME?
SURE— BECAUSE YOU'RE SO HANDSOME.
GASP
BUT, I DON'T ACTUALLY KNOW WHAT'S GOING ON! I DON'T EVEN KNOW WHAT YEAR IT IS!
HA HA HA
HA HA HA THAT'S TRUE.
OH, WELL.
HA HA HA HA
WHAT YEAR IS IT, ANYWAY, LINDA?
UM
M.K. BROWN · 2016

CARTOONS & ILLUSTRATIONS BY
R. Barrett, C. Barsotti, L. Bertman, C. Bonno, G. Booth, A. Breckman, S. Brodner, M.K. Brown, M. Bryan, R. Chast, D. Chelsea, J. Cuneo, E. Delessert, N. Downes, T. Frey, D. Friedman, M. Gerberg, A. Goldwyn, S. Gross, R. Grossman, J. Jonik, T. Hanson, F. Katz, P. Krassner, K. Krimstein, P. Kuper, P.S. Mueller, J. Oesterle, J. Plotkin, J. F. Putnam, M. Reddy, C. Shapan, M. Shiell, M. Simonson, R. Sparks, N. Spooner, B.K. Taylor, S. Torelli, A. Veve, D. Watson, A. Weldon, Wende, W. Wood and J. Ziegler.

COVER: "The Court of Donald I" by Steve Brodner.

ACKNOWLEDGMENTS

All material is ©2017 its creators, all rights reserved; please do not reproduce or distribute it without written consent of the creators and *The American Bystander*. The following material has previously appeared, and is reprinted here with permission of the author(s): Steve Brodner's cover first appeared in *The Los Angeles Times*. Armando Veve's illustration (p. 57) appeared in *New Scientist*. "Still and all, why bother? Here's my answer. Many people need desperately to receive this message: 'I feel and think much as you do, care about many of the things you care about, although most people do not care about them. You are not alone.'"—*Kurt Vonnegut*

PLEASE TAKE NOTE:

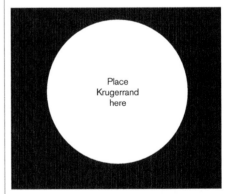

Place Krugerrand here

It has come to our attention that an international ring of counterfeiters has recently targeted the Krugerrand, the South African coin which accounts for 90% of the world's gold market. Luckily, in their mad lust for ill-gotten profit, these criminals have made one crucial error: *The copies are too small.* Authorities worldwide are on the lookout for these "Krugerrunts," and have asked us to alert our readers as a public service.

Above is the diameter of an authentic Krugerrand; **any smaller coins are worthless fakes.** Please measure your stock immediately; possession or use of these fakes may arouse the suspicion of Interpol. As a service to our readers, we are collecting these dummy coins for disposal. If any of your Krugerrands are too small, please send them to the Publisher care of this magazine and he will dispose of them for you. Boy, will he.

American Bystanders #1

THE AMERICAN BYSTANDER, *Vol. 1, No. 4*, (978-0-692-86912-3). Publishes four times a year if things break just right, otherwise, fewer. We keep it vague in order to acclimate our readership to disappointment. Dashed hopes are a big part of life, and in our experience things go better after one makes his/her peace with it. ©2017 by Good Cheer LLC. No part of this book can be reproduced, in whole or in part, by any means, without the written permission of the Publisher. For this and other queries, email *publisher@americanbystander.org*, or write: Michael Gerber, Publisher, *The American Bystander*, 1122 Sixth St., #403, Santa Monica, CA 90403. Subscribe at www.patreon.com/bystander. Other info can be found at www.americanbystander.org... if you're really into us.

JOHN CUNEO

NEWS & NOTES

This edition of N&N is dedicated to all the therapists (including my own, and perhaps **JOHN CUNEO**'s) who are sick to death of listening to everybody's Trump Anxiety Dreams.

ALAN ZWEIBEL (page 48) has five grandchildren ages 1 to 8, and none of them find him funny no matter how many times he forces them to watch videos of his TV shows and movies, read his books and act out his plays.

ETHAN PERSOFF has been recovering from post-2016 political events through a slow drip of bourbon tonics and Philip K. Dick novels. He's close to fully questioning this reality, and feels great about it. Getting away from yelling at the television news for a day, Persoff interviewed **PAUL KRASSNER** for this issue of *Bystander*. Paul's optimistic presence on these pages is a bright and wise respite from the gloom, and we're all thankful. The two recently collaborated on a coffee

table book celebrating the best cartoons of Paul's creation, *The Realist*, appropriately titled *The Realist Cartoons*, now available from Fantagraphics Books.

J.A. WEINSTEIN (@JohnnyStyne) ferried to beautiful downtown Hoboken *once again* to appear on Artie Lange's ArtieQuitter.com Podcast #367, where J.A. promulgated the riff on Artie's groundbreaking "Hogan's List" show idea. Before the festivities ended, Artie gave *Bystander* a nice little plug: "*American Bystander*, it's a comedic magazine, à la *The Onion*, with a lot of REALLY credible funny motherfuckers writing for it." Thank you, Artie — we do our best.

• • •

As I was putting the finishing touches on this issue — tormenting our copy editor with the usual flood of questionable grammar, English-as-she-is-spoke punctuation and inadvertent neologisms that is just *me bein' me* — Facebook

belched out some terrible news: Cartoonist **JACK ZIEGLER**, a contributor to *Bystander* since before the beginning, had passed away suddenly.

I'd first learned Jack was sick on Feb. 28, when his usual shipment of brilliant work had included the note, "Sorry this has taken so long but I've been ill for weeks now and not out of the woods yet." To which I responded: "I'll pass 'em around. Take good care of yourself; you are an essential man." This was no palaver: In his graceful whimsy and whimsical grace, Jack Ziegler epitomized what we're trying to do here.

When it comes to *The American Bystander*, Jack was grandfathered in. He first met our fearless leader **BRIAN McCONNACHIE** when both were six; Jack even met his first wife at Brian's wedding. According to an interview with *The Comics Journal*, it was Brian who first suggested Jack make a real go at cartooning. "I can't

(Cartoonists always want their work bigger, so here you go, Jack.)

even draw and I'm selling cartoons," Jack quoted Brian as saying. "You can actually draw. Maybe this is something you might wanna think about." So this is another thing we should all thank Brian for.

After five years of fits and starts, Jack began selling work to *The New Yorker*, and his life's work began. He would sell a prodigious number of cartoons to them, over 1,500, subtly shifting the comic sensibility of that magazine.

In 1982, Brian recruited Jack to contribute to the original *American Bystander*; so it was natural that in 2011, when I began serious discussions with Brian and **ALAN GOLDBERG** about a resurrection, I reached out to Jack. In the midst of a long conversation about the Beatles, Jack pledged "as many cartoons as you need."

It's impossible to overestimate the importance of this; if our new *Bystander*

was to be worth doing, it had to have material from the best people around — Jack was certainly that. And I knew that "Jack Ziegler" was a name to conjure with when talking to other possible contributors. Jack knew that, too, which makes his enthusiastic support even more generous. But that was him.

I can't say I knew Jack well — I hoped to, one day — but the outpouring of grief from friends online and off has demonstrated just how dear he was to so many. We will, if we're allowed, continue to print Jack's work — as we do with **CHARLEY BARSOTTI** — because I feel that the best way to honor a cartoonist is to let them keep on doing what they do best: make people laugh.

Like Arno and Addams and Hokinson and Barsotti, Jack Ziegler will go on entertaining people for as long as there's

ink on paper. Death is clearly small beer compared to Hamburger Madness. I was happy to know him, and happy to publish him, and know that Jack's being buoyed to The Next Place by a million bubbles of laughter.

COMING NEXT ISSUE: *Bystander* #5 promises to be quite useful. Because starting is the hardest part, Ed Subitzky has sent along 101 sure-fire beginnings for a novel. For those of you considering the expat life, Phil Proctor of the Firesign Theater is providing a few lessons in Latvian. The ever-sensible Ron Barrett warns against the silent killer: dangerous clothing…Plus Jack Handey and his clone; Rick Meyerowitz; and much more! Should be crowdfunded this summer. But why not beat the rush? Subscribe now at www.patreon.com/bystander. **B**

LADIES AND GENTLEMEN, **Lenny Bruce!**

In 1961, Lenny Bruce began a gig at New York's *VILLAGE VANGUARD.* His first time headlining the club:

Hello Hello!

CLAP

I DON'T UNDERSTAND how Max Gordon can pay me a grand a week to work here.

He must be a **CROOK!**

CLAP

e two jazz musicians were just there to visit Powell's andmother, who had lived on that street for decades.

DITING NORMAN MAILER

HE EARLY DAYS OF THE VOICE, we'd meet every sday at 4am to drive to the printer in New Jersey, SHEPHERD's voice on radio keeping us awake...

This was always a joyous occasion, until the week of ... *NORMAN MAILER'S FIRST COLUMN* ...

Heh.

Ha!

Heh Heh!

You fat heads!

Hi Jerry,

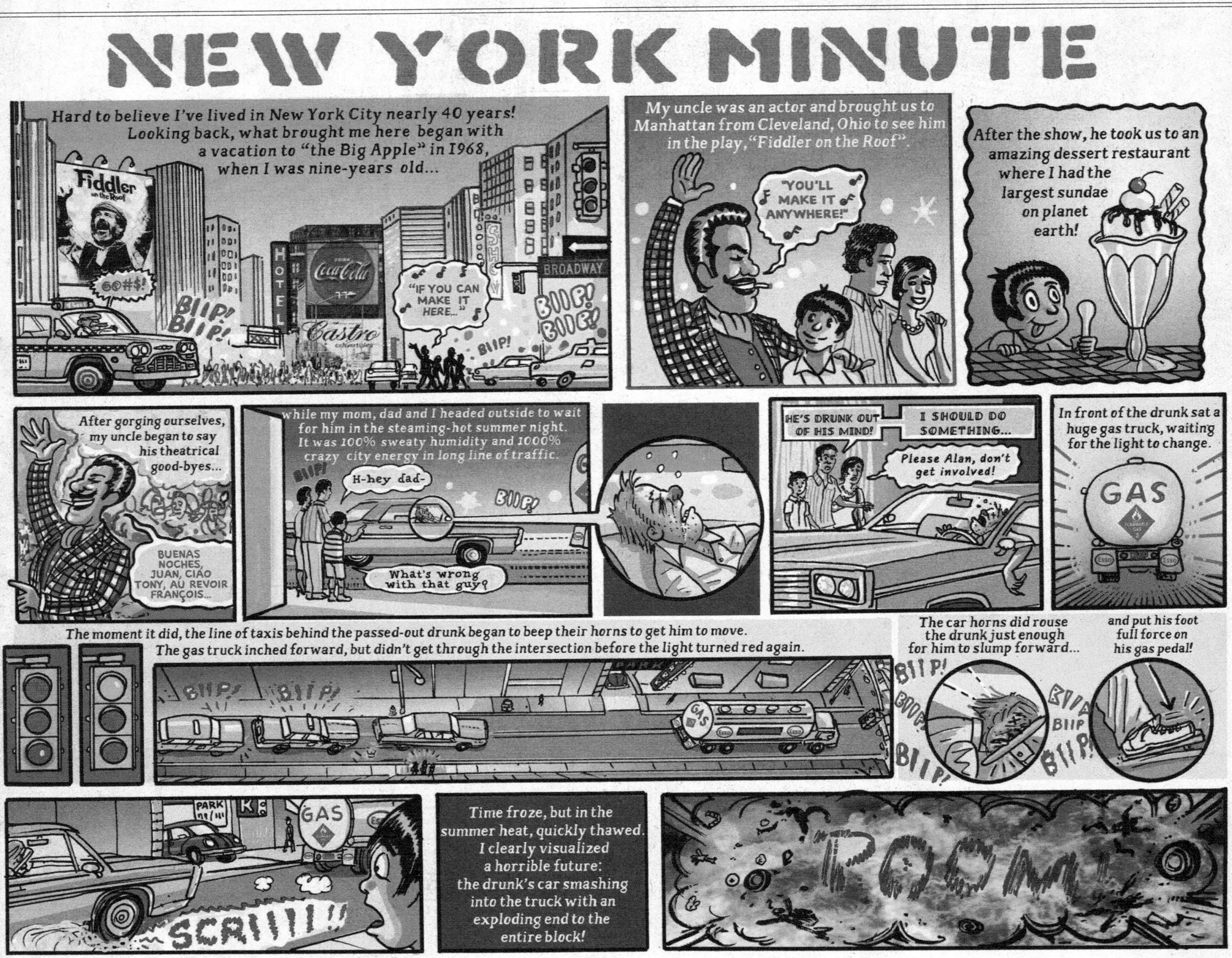
NEW YORK MINUTE
Hard to believe I've lived in New York City nearly 40 years! Looking back, what brought me here began with a vacation to "the Big Apple" in 1968, when I was nine-years old...
Fiddler on the Roof
GO#$!
BIIP! BIIP!
HOTEL
Coca-Cola
Castro
"IF YOU CAN MAKE IT HERE..."
BROADWAY
BIIP!
BIIP! BIIP!
My uncle was an actor and brought us to Manhattan from Cleveland, Ohio to see him in the play, "Fiddler on the Roof".
"YOU'LL MAKE IT ANYWHERE!"
After the show, he took us to an amazing dessert restaurant where I had the largest sundae on planet earth!
After gorging ourselves, my uncle began to say his theatrical good-byes...
BUENAS NOCHES, JUAN, CIAO TONY, AU REVOIR FRANÇOIS...
while my mom, dad and I headed outside to wait for him in the steaming-hot summer night. It was 100% sweaty humidity and 1000% crazy city energy in long line of traffic.
BIIP!
H-hey dad-
BIIP!
What's wrong with that guy?
HE'S DRUNK OUT OF HIS MIND!
I SHOULD DO SOMETHING...
Please Alan, don't get involved!
In front of the drunk sat a huge gas truck, waiting for the light to change.
GAS
The moment it did, the line of taxis behind the passed-out drunk began to beep their horns to get him to move.
The gas truck inched forward, but didn't get through the intersection before the light turned red again.
BIIP! BIIP!
PARK
GAS
The car horns did rouse the drunk just enough for him to slump forward...
BIIP! BIIP! BIIP! BIIP! BIIP!
and put his foot full force on his gas pedal!
PARK
GAS
SCRIIIII!!
Time froze, but in the summer heat, quickly thawed. I clearly visualized a horrible future: the drunk's car smashing into the truck with an exploding end to the entire block!
BOOM!

PETER KUPER (@PKuperArt) has created over two dozen books including Ruins, which won the Eisner Award for best graphic novel in 2016. He is a visiting professor at Harvard University.

Gallimaufry

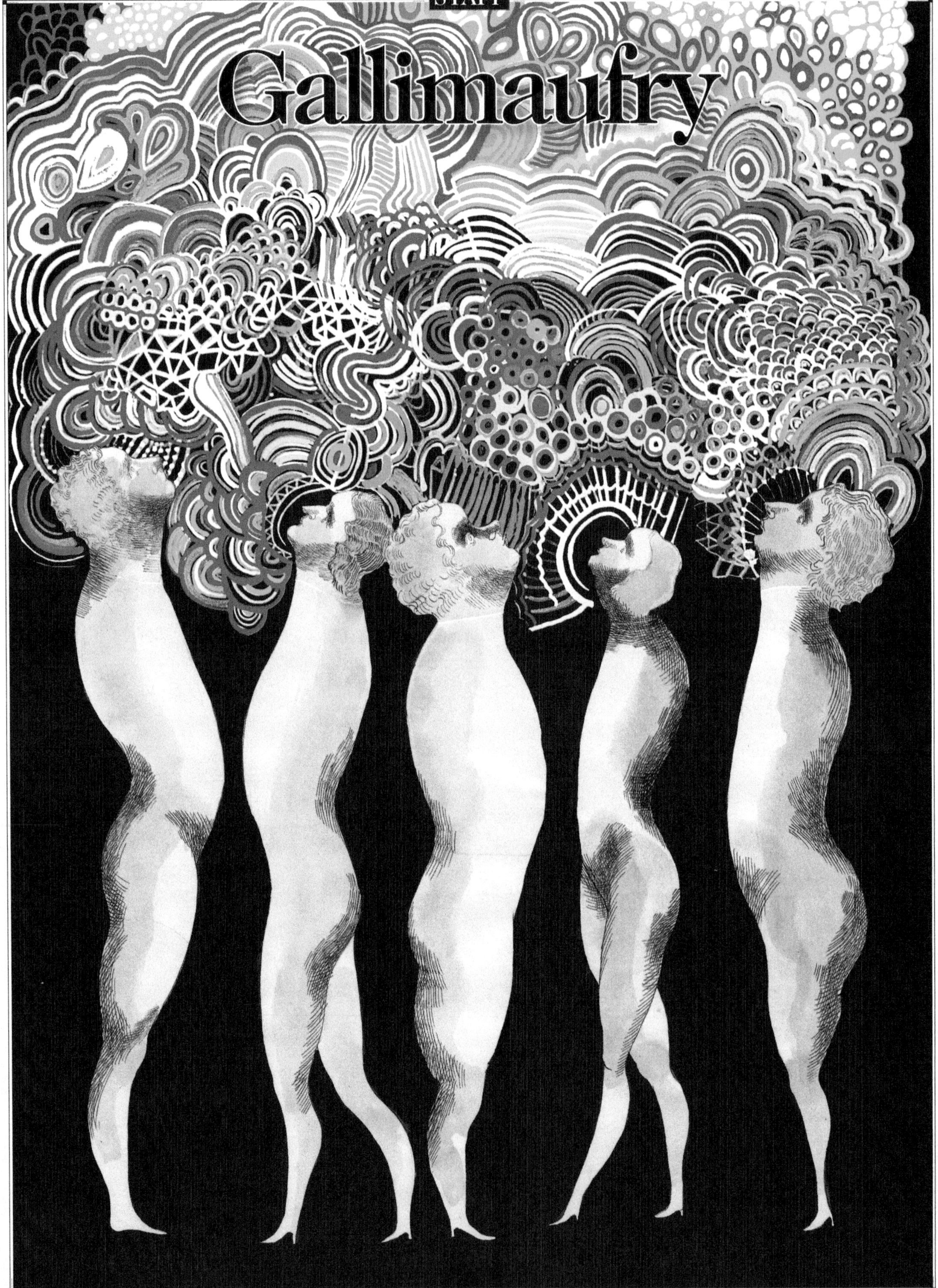

TREASURE FREY

THIS IS JUST TO RESPOND.

So you've eaten
the plums
I put in
the icebox

which I was
(and you knew this)
saving
for breakfast

This is why
you have no friends,
this and all the other
passive-aggressive bullshit

—*James Finn Garner*

NOTES ON THE PAPERBACK EDITION.

Readers of the hardcover edition of this book may notice a few changes and corrections in this new printing; the most significant are listed below.

The hardcover price was misprinted; an additional two dollars must be sent to me c/o the publisher.

"About the Author" now correctly states that I won a Baskin-Robbins coupon in a pinewood derby at the age of eight. The statement that I shot down six Iraqi helicopters has been removed. Boo-boo all better, FBI?

The hardcover edition was dedicated "to my radiant muse Emily." Please forget *that* was ever there. This book is now dedicated to whoever gets me my DVDs and my cat back.

In the two years since publication, I have made some major breakthroughs in therapy. As a result, the demonic "Vater Adolf" is no longer a caricature of my father, but has been heavily rewritten into a multilayered character with motivations actually connected to the plot.

Several people have written to ask how Lady Bingham knew that Paolo's revolver was not loaded in Chapter Eight, as the only people he had confessed this to were either off-ship in Lisbon, or steerage passengers whom Bingham was unlikely to meet, much less discuss firearms with, in the two days since she boarded the *R.M.S.*

Belligerent Duchess. The confrontation scene has been revised, to clarify that Lady Bingham has X-ray vision.

The character of police Inspector Rothschild has changed now that I've had more time to research criminal law and police procedure. Rothschild no longer calls in "special Police airstrikes," thinks up new laws to suit his immediate needs, or brandishes a graymarket dirty bomb the size of a pen. (In this edition, it's just a pen.) Also, a friend told me what "virulent" means, so the passage about Rothschild searching virulently for the stolen dossier has been deleted.

One review of the book called it a "tiresome rehash of the hackneyed Victorian murder-mystery genre," which on reflection I kind of agree with, so where possible I have reconfigured the story as a cyberpunk thriller. This makes the largest difference during the conundrum of the locked billiard room in Chapter 14, which is now an attempt to bypass the firewall of China's largest manufacturer of the maxidepressant drug "Skag" by jacking the neural implants of Killerwatt, the brainwashed keyboardist of Neo-York's leading crimecore band, Battery, into the OmniBrane via the restored MUNI-SURV terminal retrieved from the sunken remains of Staten Island — but the change is noticeable in other places as well.

Following complaints by Asian-American groups, the character "Chop-Chop" has been renamed "Dr. Jeffrey Wu," and all dialect has been removed. Lady Bingham's adventure among the Goola-Goola Men of Darkest Zambolia has also been cut. Please stop tweeting me.

Many readers have complained that the recipe for lemon chiffon cake in Chapter 30 resulted in an inedible sludge that damaged their bakeware. I don't know what to tell you; the book is clearly labeled as fiction. Chef René also jumped on a charging rhino's back in Chapter 33, but I didn't get pissy letters about that.

Finally, the original epilogue contained a small but significant typo: The names "Vasilios" and "Drexler" were switched, reversing the fates that befell those characters. As a result of this small change, the book is no longer an inspiring triumph of human resilience, as celebrated by the UN's first-ever "World Reads Day," but a dour and depressing portrait of the universe's blithe indifference to the fiddling concerns of a few shaved apes squatting on a rock hurtling through space. The various Utopian movements inspired by the hardcover edition are advised to adjust their mission statements accordingly. Also: Kick out Emily. Turns out, she totally didn't get it.

—*Tim Harrod*

"Now I have another reason to hate clowns."

THINGS OTHER THAN KRYPTONITE THAT MAKE SUPERMAN FEEL ALL TOO HUMAN.

Forgetting trash day
Flying through spiderwebs
Trying to drink from a beer boot
Super-acne
Blanking on the name of someone he just met
Removing a bra
Keeping track of receipts
A Rubik's cube
Trying to make a decent béarnaise
February

—Michael Thornton

A BOUQUET OF HAIKU.

Stalling
Okay here we go
Give me a sec to warm up
Poem on the way

Procrastination
This was due today?
Um window chair computer
Stack of mail wallet

Distraction
Facebook Twitter Yelp
X-Box PC tennis ball
Puppy screensaver

Regret
Those were bad haikus
It was wrong to waste your time
Should have wrote better

—Evan Waite

MY BUCKET LIST.

According to my doctor, I have the heartbeat of a 17-year-old. And the blood pressure, and the reflexes. "Something is going to kill you," he wheezes, double-checking a chart, "but I sure can't find it. Yet." My doctor is an incredibly fat man, which makes it easier to hear him openly rooting for my cause of death.

He may get there before me, but we're all headed to the same destination: Eternity. And nowadays, in our culture of maximum achievement, between Here and Eternity is a pretty exhausting trip.

According to a popular series of books, before you die there are at least 1000 Places to See, Foods to Eat, Records to Hear, Beers to Drink, Movies to Watch, Video Games to Play, TV Shows to Enjoy, Paintings to View, Cars to Drive, and Guitars to Play. And the internet, predictably, provides even more lists.

All this pretty much guarantees that someday I'll be lying in bed, my adolescent's heart beating its last, croaking bitterly to some unlucky relation: "I should've had flesh-eating fish give me a pedicure! Why did I not kitesurf Malawi? I never went zorbing!"[1]

So, in a world full of "must-dos", I have whittled it down to the following customized ten:

1. "Write something that changes someone's day." It might be a love letter. Or it might be a note that begins, "I have a weapon. Put all of your small bills in this sack…"
2. "Achieve your ideal weight." On Jupiter. As a 160-pound person, that means plumping up to about 380. Sure, I might feel a little self-conscious at first, but I'll look positively svelte next to the Great Red Spot.
3. "Get a tattoo." But it's cheating if you remember how or why. Foghorn Leghorn seems like a good choice of image to discover in the shower. I will

---

[1] Zorbing is rolling down a hill in a big plastic ball. Throw in a demon with a pitchfork, and you've got a perfect hipster Hell.

forever be a Man of Mystery, even to myself.
4. "Try a different profession." "Sky Mall Entrepreneur" sounds good. Lipitor Chip ice cream, extreme aromatherapy, paparazzi sticks, crawling desks — only a couple of these products need to hit!
5. "Teach a child." To smoke.
6. "Develop a memory like an elephant." Think I can cross this one off already. "Walked around, ate grass off the veldt, thought about screwing elephants some more" — what's the big deal?
7. "Start today on your bucket list." But like I said, there are a lot, so I'm planning to multitask. I won't just learn to play chess, and swim with a manatee; I'll play chess with the manatee! I'll have a romantic dinner on an iceberg. I'll donate blood on a Slip 'N Slide. I'll dance in the rain while parachuting to Machu Picchu. I'll beat up a leprechaun (okay, that's still one thing, but it sounds like fun).
8. "Do a perfect pushup." Okay, but only if I can bitch about it for weeks.
9. "Write an autobiography." Yes — someone else's. I'll be fearless about disclosing the shortcomings and regrets. I will practice radical honesty.
10. "Visit a childhood friend." In the age of Facebook? You can't get rid of them. I'll stick to visiting imaginary playmates. We'll laugh together reading my doctor's obituary.

And if there's any more time… I'll demand a rematch with the manatee. This time, I'll cheat.

—Quentin Hardy

SIGNS THAT YOU MAY INDEED SMELL LIKE PORRIDGE.

You're frequently hassled by movie theater personnel, convinced you swiped a hot dog/fries/porridge Combo Deal.

Who are they calling Goldilocks? You're a brunette!

That time you escaped from prison, the cops had the bloodhounds sniff a bowl of you-know-what.

Your sister is determined to set you up with her friend who "totally stinks like maple syrup."

After you win Eurovision, your signature cologne is ...gloppy.

When you spill large amounts of porridge onto your shirt, NOBODY NOTICES.

—Kit Lively

HOMER'S CATALOG OF SHIPS.

***120' Trireme**. Battle-ready. Original varnish. Salt-and-sea-spray-proofed with 100% guarantee.*

This commanding war vessel has had only one prior owner: a little old lady who used it on Sundays to go to church. Just picture it: 50 wooden oars bobbing up and down in the hands of brand-new rowing slaves, their groans barely audible, accelerating so fast that, before you can even recite the epode to the Iliad, you've gone from zero to six. Now picture yourself at the helm. Isn't that where you belong?

***8' Rowboat.** Three oars. Battle flag. Six small holes in hull.*

This fixer-upper is a little boat with a lot of heart — and a story to tell. Its last owner, an Achaean chieftain, used it to battle the fabled Kraken of the deep. But wait — is that real teak siding? No, but your friends won't notice.

***60' Sporting Craft**. Alone or in bulk set of 12. Freshly painted.*

Perfect for a leisurely trip homeward from abroad — so perfect, in fact, you may be a decade or two late for dinner! It's the ideal home away from home: Everything about this sleek black clipper says style. The solid wooden mast comes with a free rigging, handy for all types of sail, as well as for lashing yourself to the ship — we won't judge. Accommodates a crew of as many as 50, or — in case everyone you know is slowly killed off by witches, monsters, and angry gods — as few as one.

If you would like to own any of these quality pre-loved ships at yesterday's prices, contact Blind Homer (sales associate) at 1-900-OLD-SHIP by telephone or Telemachus.

—Daniel Galef

TALK TO THE HAND.

—Steve Brodner

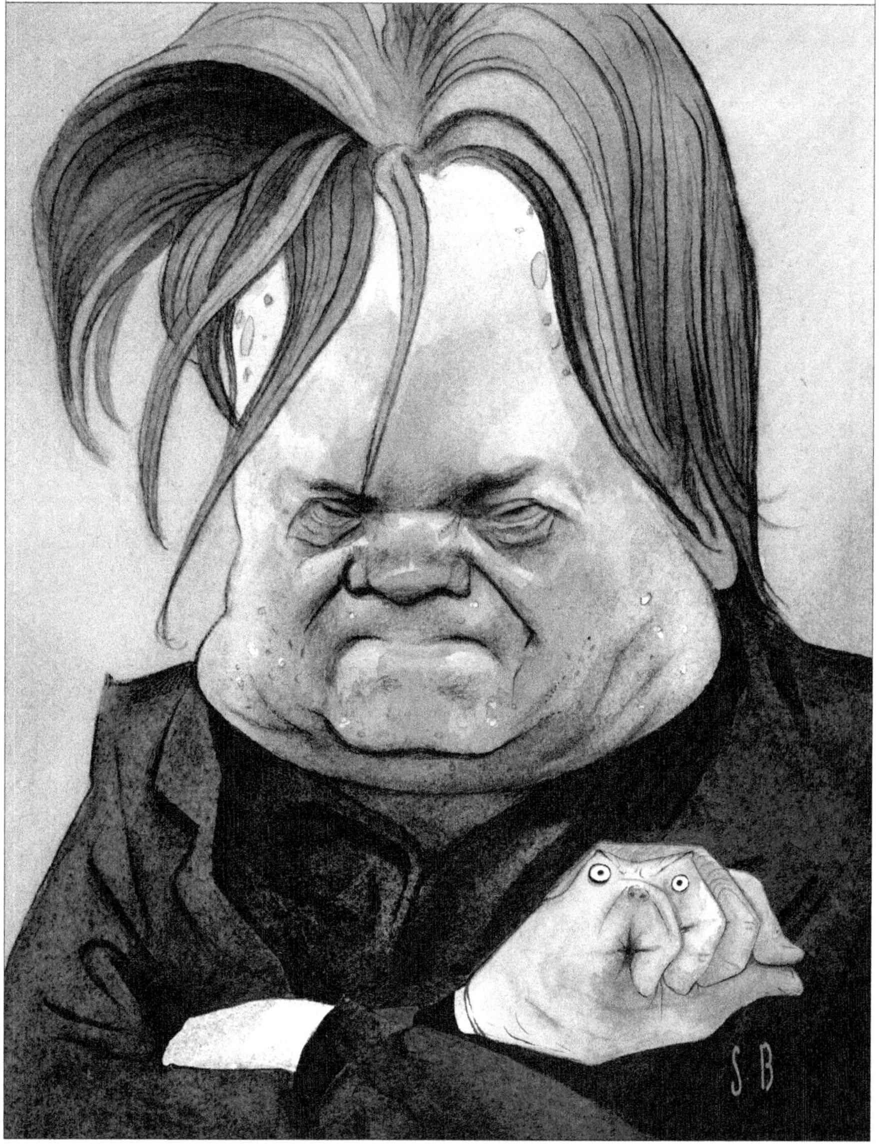

SB

PEOPLE WHO DIED TOO YOUNG.

Kurt Cobain
Jesus Christ
River Phoenix
Anne Frank
Amy Winehouse
Joan of Arc
Corey Haim
John F, Kennedy
You

—Larry Doyle

PEABODY'S RADICAL HISTORY

SHERMAN: Where are we going today, Mr. Peabody?

PEABODY: Sherman, set the Wayback Machine to 1921. We're going to exonerate Sacco and Vanzetti.

SHERMAN: Wow! Cause célèbre!

PEABODY (V.O.): Sherman did as I instructed and soon we were in the Massachusetts courtroom.

JUDGE: I hereby sentence you two anarchists to —

PEABODY (interrupting): Excuse me, Judge.

JUDGE: Who are you?

PEABODY: Peabody's the name. And this is my pet boy, Sherman.

SHERMAN: Hi!

JUDGE: Pleasure to meet you both, but this is a trial!

PEABODY: More of a mistrial, Your Honor. The only thing Sacco and Vanzetti are guilty of is bad fashion sense.

FATHERLY ADVICE

Andy Breckman, 2017

SHERMAN: They do look pretty grubby!
PEABODY: Quiet, Sherman.
JUDGE: What evidence do you have?
PEABODY (V.O.): I patiently dismantled the state's case, pointing out the contradictions in testimonies and timelines, shoddy ballistic tests and compromised sources. I then gave a brief summation of European libertarian communism and its role in the American radical theory. I also reminded them that I was from the future. Judge, jury and counsel stood to applaud my declamation.
JUDGE: I gotta say, Mr. Peabody, that was one convincing argument!
PEABODY: More like several arguments, Judge, but thank you all the same.
JUDGE (bangs gavel): The defendants are free to go!
SACCO: Thanka you, Mr. Peabodies!
VANZETTI: Now we are-a free to agitate for a living wage-a!
SHERMAN: You did it again, Mr. Peabody!
PEABODY: Naturally. Only one thing bothers me.
SHERMAN: What's that?
PEABODY: Vanzetti's pants. His tailor should be on trial.
SHERMAN: And the charge?
PEABODY: A stitch that's a crime gets you nine.
(Sour tuba sting)

—*Dennis Perrin*

HOLDING PATTERN.

As did those preceding it, 2016 proved a year of constant defeat and disgrace, with some new humiliation attending me on what seemed a daily basis. Chief among these markers of my decline was my continued failure to be published in *Hemispheres*, the official in-flight magazine of United Airlines.

Though I am an accomplished essayist whose work has been featured on several prominent blogging platforms, Hemispheres remains the dew-slicked plum dangling just beyond my trembling grasp, taunting me with its untasted juices. Once again, I submitted several pieces to *Hemispheres* — and once again, I was bludgeoned to the dirt and spat upon by the wards of this Hall of Heroes, who permitted me neither entry nor dignity. Here are my rejected pitches:

Terror In the Skies—This exposé reveals the mounting instances of "sudden failure" in commercial air fleets around the world, most occurring on airplanes that "seemed fine." Painstakingly researched, this important, indeed essential article demonstrates what I call "the deadly gamble" of air travel, with the only bulwark against catastrophe being crews of enervated, underpaid avionics technicians whose senses are constantly flooded by the hideous shrieking of dozens of jet engines.

Surfin' and Turfin' — A direct and forthright meal attainment guide addressing the best steak-seafood combos among the nation's eateries. I feel that this piece echoes precisely many similar Fine Dining columns I have studied in the stacks of *Hemispheres* back issues filling my apartment, excepting the final sentence, in which it is noted that people who occupy themselves with tracking down good surf and turf tend to be complete fucking assholes.

The Business Traveler — Though sex thrillers aren't a common feature of in-flight magazines, I was convinced that the editors would be tempted by the steamy, refreshingly graphic descriptions of vaginal intercourse peppering my tale of a midlevel pharm rep who meets an exotic but murderous temptress through a matchmaking service advertised in Hemispheres itself. The novella ends with the lothario's personal and professional ruination, a fate no more shameful than being curtly informed by email that, "this has gone on for long enough," and that, "[my] future submissions [would] be discarded without being read."

The Business Traveler 2: Flyin' High — A sequel to the previous sex thriller, which I submitted prior to receiving rejection of the first, admittedly an unforced error. This installment features even steamier, more fluid-rich intimacy, as well as a compelling scene where, needing to burn an incriminating love letter during a redeye from LAX to PHL, the protagonist enters the 757's lavatory and disables its smoke detector.

Jordan Heller: Portrait of Evil — Another research piece, this one dragging into the naked sunlight the incompetence and moral desolation of *Hemispheres* editor in chief Jordan Heller. Drawing on work featured on several prominent blogging platforms, as well as interviews with dozens of sources whose anonymity I have sworn to uphold, this 10,000-word article concludes that Heller lacks the editorial judgment to lead *Hemispheres*, and calls for his immediate resignation and/or pummeling.

The Iron Horse — This serendipitous feature resulted from a rail trip from Peoria to New York City I was forced to take after my name somehow appeared on the FBI's No-Fly List. Though shaking with rage throughout much of the Rust Belt, I found surcease in the soothing rumble of the undercarriage, concluding in my article that Amtrak is vastly superior to any cramped, turbulent plane ride — and comparably priced! Though it is worth noting that my sense of calm explosively dissipated at the moment I arrived at my destination: the *Hemispheres* editorial offices.

These are my failures. While each one seared me, I hope that by confessing them in this public forum, I can wipe the slate clean. With luck, as well as with a pseudonym and a different font, I firmly believe that *Hemispheres* will this year grant me entrance into the Hall. In that silvered mausoleum my work will be entombed, my readers both informed and entertained as they sip ginger ale and nibble on miniature pretzel coils, shimmering motes suspended in that quiet ether between Earth and Christ we know as the friendly skies.

—*Django Gold*

JEWISH-THEMED WESTERNS.

Jew Grit
High Noon-ish
The Treasury Bonds of Sierra Madre
The Sedentary Bunch

Two Mohels for Sister Sara
Shanela
Rio Mazel
The Pretty Good Six
Butch Cassidy and the Other Handsome Guy, What's-His-Name? Blond With the Mustache
Django Uncircumcised
For a Few Dollars Less
The In-Law Josey Wales
Pale Miser
Once Upon a Time in the Vest Business
High Plains Assessor
Lower Back Pain Mountain
She Leased a Yellow Ribbon
Hang'em High Enough
The Long Discussion at the OK Corral
The Man Who Managed Liberty Valance
A Fistful of Challahs

—*Arnie & Jay Kogen*

FUNNY MONEY.

Our country is teetering on the brink of disaster for one obvious reason: Our currency is in complete disarray.

George Washington's picture graces the front of the one-dollar bill because he's our first president, which makes perfect sense. But George Washington's face is also on the quarter. It should be on the penny to match.

But the penny bears a profile of Abraham Lincoln, whose image is also on the five-dollar bill. His picture should be on the nickel to match. But on the nickel is a portrait of Thomas Jefferson, whose face also appears on the two-dollar bill—even though Jefferson was our third president.

Take a look in your wallet; it's total anarchy in there. The ten-dollar bill features a picture of Alexander Hamilton, who never served as president at all; Hamilton was secretary of the Treasury. That's just wrong on so many levels. The ten-dollar bill should depict our tenth president, John Tyler, who should also be on the dime to match. But on the dime is a picture of Franklin D. Roosevelt, who was our 32nd president. And what an insult to FDR! The dime is smaller than the nickel, and even smaller than the penny. The dime should be the penny, the penny should be the nickel, and the nickel should be the dime.

On the twenty-dollar bill, we've got a portrait of Andrew Jackson, who was our seventh president. The twenty should obviously feature our twentieth president, James Garfield. "Hold on there," you're saying to yourself. "This is America. Presidents like Abraham Lincoln and John F. Kennedy—assassinated people—should be on the money." Well, James Garfield was assassinated, so that's good news. And instead of having George Washington on the quarter, we should use our 25th president, William McKinley—who, as luck would have it, was

Viking Funeral

assassinated, too. Perfect.

The fifty-dollar bill depicts Ulysses S. Grant, who was our eighteenth president, which makes absolutely no sense. We haven't even elected a fiftieth president yet. So, we should take Ronald Reagan, put his picture on a forty-dollar bill, and together with John Tyler on a ten-dollar bill — *voilà!* — you've got fifty bucks.

Our hundred shows Benjamin Franklin, who was also never president. He was too busy flying a kite in a lightning storm. The man could have been killed. That's not the role model we want for our children. That's like putting Evel Knievel or the Flying Wallendas on the one-hundred-dollar bill. And, of course, there hasn't yet been a hundredth president of the United States. So we could take the two George Bushes — that's 41 and 43 — add them together, and that totals 84. That means we need 16 more, which gives us our sixteenth president, Abraham Lincoln. So we take a picture of Abraham Lincoln, Photoshop him with his arms around the two George Bushes, and we've got one hundred bucks. Problem solved.

This is clearly our country's most promising economic stimulus plan. Write to your senators and congressman so we can fix this mess. America, you'll be left with plenty of money to burn. That's a guarantee.

—*Joey Green*

THE SEVEN DEADLY SINS (VIA FACEBOOK).

Gluttony — Finally snagged reservations at Bisnonno! LOOK at this famous 6-ft prosciutto-covered prosciutto sandwich! They bring it to the table instead of breadsticks, and you can get as many as you want. Appetizers are like eating an orgasm, entrees are HUMONGOUS. I took a photo of dessert (chocolate porkfat volcano, obvs) but my fingers were too greasy to work the panorama function.

Sloth — Dare you NOT to check out "37,241 Insane Facts About 'Ferris Bueller's Day Off'." Did you know that, throughout the entire shoot, Broderick never changed underpants? Or that Nell Carter was originally cast to play Ferris's mom? WARNING: This destroyed my whole afternoon! Who knew squandering the precious gift of life could be SO. MUCH. FUN.

Pride — Happy to announce that I have just been named Tilden and Associates' senior-junior associate vice president, leading a talented team of associates, who will in turn lead their own talented teams of associates. I start the gig next week, when new hubby and I return from Tulum... heaven! #feelingblessed

Envy — Mad props to my best friend Maggie, who just became Tilden's new senior-junior manager vice president. This is such great news for her! So proud of Maggie, nothing stops you

(Thad, nail fungus, IBS)! Lean in, girl!

Greed — Guysies, CHECK THIS: 19c ship captain's house, renovated to look new in 1982, then renovated to look old in 2011. Pond in back, stream in front, and a river (w/fish!) circling the house in the manner of a medieval moat. Artists' barn on the property can be converted into a third home, for whenever I get sick of the second home. W-A-N-T!

Wrath — DC has finally gone TOO FAR. Sign this Change.org petition to force Congress to fund a rocket ship that will carry all of its 535 members into outer space and deposit them on the surface of the sun. #burnCongressburn

Lust — Late-night selfie! #paintingthetown #lookingfeisty #meow

—*Jay Ruttenberg*

MENCKEN MOUSE.

Who's the leader of the club for caustic commentary?
M-E-N, C-K-E-N, M-O-U-S-E!

Journalist and humorist from the 20th century!
M-E-N, C-K-E-N, M-O-U-S-E!
Mencken Mooouuuse... Mencken Mooouuuse...
Forever let us hold forth bitter bile!
(*shouted*) Bile! Bile! Bile!
Come along and join the song that's so curmudgeonly!
M-E-N, C-K-E-N, M-O-U-S-E!
(*softly*)
M-E-N-C...

(*spoken*) See you real soon!
K-E-N...
(*spoken*) E-N? Because contrarian.
Emmm, ohhh, youu, esss, eeeee.
--*phin*--

—*Todd Hanson*

THE MUSEUM OF YOUR FAMILY REUNION.

Welcome! Please press "one" on your audio guides to continue in English, "two" to continue in Mom's English (Screaming), and "three" for a vicious, personal, "just what you DIDN'T want to hear" insult to begin your visit in the traditional manner.

Thank you for selecting "three." What a terrible idea. But then again, what do you know about good life choices? Three shitty jobs in two years, can't keep a boyfriend...you throw yourself at one guy after the other, and they stay just long enough to realize what a trainwreck you are. Stop crying, you know it's true.

Tissues are available behind every plaque. Now, onto the exhibits!

The first painting on your left is entitled, *How Many Times Do I Have To Tell You: Not While We Are Eating* (2011). This evocative piece dates back to when you and your sister received iPhones, after promising you would never become addicted to them. In dramatic, Fauvist colors, it shows your mother yelling in the middle of a nice restaurant: "OUR FAMILY HASN'T SPOKEN IN YEARS BECAUSE OF YOUR ADDICTIONS. That's right, I said *addictions*. You know Julie, from yoga? Her kids don't look at their phones unless they ring. Maybe I failed as a parent." In the corner, the artist has added the small, almost stabbing figure of your father, whose expression seems to say, "Yes, Mindy. Yes, you did."

Just to the right, you can see a small Caran d'Ache study for this painting, on loan from the Getty. It is called (rather ominously given the later work), *I Don't Care What Julie Lets Her Kids Do. I Am Not Julie* (2010).

As you walk further down this hall, you will find a self-portrait by your grandmother: *That's The Tie You Want To Dress My Son In?* (2016) A provoca-tive, almost combative piece, we see your grandmother facing the viewer, while holding an admittedly very mediocre piece of neckwear. Her expression is direct to the point of causing pain; this is typical of the artist, who often betrays a sharp judgment of your decisions through piercing eyes. These signature eyes also appear in your grandmother's earlier works, *Thanksgiving* (2012) and *Thanksgiving* (2013), both oil-on-linen. The former displays your grandmother holding a mediocre pie; the latter, a mediocre turkey. Because, of course, your mother cannot do anything right. (And nor, it is implied in powerful brushstrokes, can you.)

As you exit this room, please press "four" for advice on whether to take the elevator to the next exhibit or not.

Thank you for pressing "four." At your age, we used to only use stairs. Not only that, but we loved using stairs. Millennials are so out-of-shape.

Please walk up the stairs on your left to continue.

Once you have caught your breath, on your immediate right, you will see an exhibit of contemporary pieces, created by the modernist duo, your mother and your father.

Straight ahead on the back wall is a mural by your father powerfully titled, *When You're Older You'll Stop This Communism* (2016). The pieces directly to its left are the two-part lithograph prints by your mother called, *And Who Was The Genius Who Brought Up Politics?* (2016) and *The Same Person That Brings Up Work On Weekends* (2016). Etched with dramatic chiaroscuro, the diptych features tense glares from the adult nieces and nephews, an exhausted self-portrait of your mother, an apologetic glance from the children of your privileged uncle; and that cousin's face midscream as he reveals his shirt reading "STILL FEEL THE BERN."

Before you leave, it may be worth spending a few minutes with our final piece. This exhibit is the world premiere of a careful tableau orchestrated by your quiet brother entitled, *Enough! Remember When We Used To Enjoy Each Other's Company? We Had So Much Fun Together. It Was Back When Us Kids Were Young, When The Adults Were Still Excited To See Each Other. Don't You All Miss It? Why Can't We Just Have Fun Like We Used To? Why Is Everything So Tense? Why Does Every Dinner Have to End With Some Horrible, Painful Insults? Why Does Every Little Thing Mean Something Bigger About Our Personalities Or Lifestyles? Why Are We All So Critical? Mom, Stop Telling Dad He's Not Doing Anything For This Family. He Is. Dad, Stop Telling Mom She's Being A Harpy. Grandma, Mom Shouldn't Have To Keep Working For Your Approval. She's Here To Stay. I'm Sick of This Family. Until You Guys Get Your*

"I know, I know — don't go shopping when you're hungry."

Shit Together, I'm Not Coming Back To Any More Reunions (2016).

A major departure from the family oeuvre, only time will tell if this strong and perceptive work heralds a new direction. If you're asking me, I wouldn't bet on it.

As you exit, we would like to thank you so much for taking this time to visit the Museum of Your Family Reunion. We hope it was horrible and then almost fun, and then horrible again, ending in horrible, painful insults. Please pick up a brochure for 2017's highly anticipated summer show by your quiet Brother: "Okay, I'm Back But I Can Explain."

—*Broti Gupta*

GETTING IN FRONT OF IT.

Before everything is leaked to the crooked media, I want to come clean about the *kompromat* Russian intelligence has on me:

1. Those are not my real calves. They're implants.
2. But those *are* my real boobs.
3. I'm not actually half Jewish. It's more like 60/40.
4. All the urine found on the beds of my hotel rooms sadly belongs to me.

—*Mike Shear*

DEAR NASA, I'D LIKE TO FIGHT AN ALIEN.

Dear NASA, You don't know me, but I'm a longtime fan of your organization and its various missions. Congratulations on the Moon landing and my condolences on the lost rovers.

I'm writing to make a specific request: I would like to fight an alien.

Let me start with my qualifications: I'm a U.S. taxpayer, and I'm excellent at fighting. I've gotten into at least two bar brawls every weekend since I was 18 (I'm 27 now). After nearly 1,000 fights, I'm getting pretty darn bored of fighting other humans. Just to switch it up I've battled most of the appliances in my home, but it's hard to tell who wins. I tipped over the dishwasher and broke its utensil basket. I took on a midsized car, and we tied on a technicality when it ran out of gas. It's all been unsatisfying. I'm ready for a fresh challenge, and what better 1,000th opponent than a space creature? Whether it be tentacled, slimy, scaled, or made of pure gas, whatever form, I just want the chance to try and pummel the little freak into the dust.

Going toe-to-toe, or toe-to-whatever-those-alien-guys-got is my dream fight. But beyond personal reasons, this fight could benefit NASA. How else can we see how little green men react to my stout grapple, my famed left hook, or my flailing kick once I've fallen down? How else will we know how aliens respond to me tweaking their weird elephant noses?

Imagine the scientific knowledge to be gained! How do aliens cheer each other on or throw chairs around when they fight? Do they even have concepts like cheering, booing or throwing chairs around, the three cornerstones of human behavior? What sort of weird intoxicants do the aliens ingest before a fight? Do they have stimulants or depressants similar to the cocktail of whiskey and slaps to the face that I use before I "get down"?

This fight would also be a great cultural exchange. What better way to share our Earth values than to get scrappy on a plot of grass and dirt in my backyard, within a rough circle scratched out with a stick? What better way to let the aliens know what humans are all about than a sweaty contest where I try to pin down the alien's arms/legs/flesh wheels, and wail on its thorax?

I know I'm not the only one who wants to fight an alien. So why should I be the one picked to strip down and get wild? As I said, I'm an experienced fighter. I've been in tons of fistfights and scuffles with everyone and everything, from neighbors to family, fire hydrants to my diabetes, and I've always walked away with my head held high. I even fought one lady, which I try to avoid, but I had no choice after she kept coming at me. She beat my ass, so I made her my wife. Who better than me to outmaneuver many tentacles and land a clean high-kick to a big, blobby ET head?

It should go without saying that I want this to be fair. No weapons allowed. I can't use my brass knuckles, and the alien can't use their laser knuckles. Obviously, we'll both have to be naked. Whatever this alien's

RECYCLED FRAGMENT OF THE TRUE CROSS

body is working with and whatever my body's working with, that's all we're bringing to this brawl. I'm even willing to shave all my hair if the alien is hairless. Anything to make it fair.

Obviously there's a question: What are we fighting for? Me, I'll fight for nothing. You know that. But if the alien needs stakes, you guys can do whatever you need to do, I'll sign whatever, I just want to fight. If I lose, I'll go back to their home world and be their slave; my wife is cool with it. She wants me to follow my dream: to fist-tango with a freaky alien.

Boy, if you NASA guys let me, I'll do us all proud and stomp this Moon bozo into our good Earth soil. Let's make my 1,000th fight a giant leap for mankind. *Are you in?!*

—*James Folta*

WHAT SOME PEOPLE THINK.

The legs of angels, adult angels, the ones with great legs, are made of mashed potatoes. Their legs are, not the rest of them. How divine is that?!
—*B. McConnachie*

BABE RUTH BADER GINSBURG:

"The only real game, I think, in the world is judicial activism."
—*J.A. Weinstein (@JohnnyStyne)*

STEVE TORELLI

"*Someday a real rain will come and wash all the scum off the street. But today, expect occasional sprinkles.*"

Nick Downes

THE NEWEST NEW YORK CITY NEIGHBORHOODS.

TriBeCa and SoHo. NoLita and DUMBO. Everyone knows about the old new New York City neighborhoods. But what of the up-and-coming areas, the very newest of the new New York City neighborhoods? Buyers and renters take note:

SALIVA (*Streets Around Little Italy and Vicinity — You Been to Angelo's?*) If you have a taste for the pungent, SALIVA is for you. This neighborhood begins somewhere beneath the Williamsburg Bridge, and seeps west until you don't like the shops anymore. Goose your palate with the wines of Italy and the culinary fare of Chinatown as you breathe in the designer perfumes, aromatherapy candles, and scented room sprays of SoHo. Ponder the lengths to which your ancestors went to move out of the five-story tenement of your desires. SALIVA truly is a formerly rent-controlled cafeteria for the senses!

NoMoOLa (*North Moore Over to Lafayette*) Once a home to light industry, this district — which radiates outward from North Moore, crossing White Street on its way to Lafayette — is now home to the business executives and financial wizards who can both pay the unregulated loft space rents and appreciate the whimsical architectural touches left behind by the earlier wave of artist occupants who gave NoMoOLa its name.

CloTH (*Closer Than Hartford*) CloTH may be a landlocked neighborhood bounded on all sides by Astoria, but for apartment seekers from out-of-state looking to shorten the workday commute, CloTH allows residents to boast "it's only 15 minutes door-to-door to Roosevelt Island if an express train making skip stops arrives just as you reach the platform." It's a dream come true for those with excellent timing who work on Roosevelt Island! On the weekends, stroll hand in hand with your exotic lover down boulevards of discount leather coat outlets and automobile parts distributors waiting to be discovered. Return home with your treasures to large living spaces with easy-care linoleum walls inside/easy-care green painted concrete outside.

StUMBLES (*Stretch of Unlit Malodorous Bars on a Lollygag down the East Side*) Second Avenue from the Low 30s to 14th Street earned its name in the days just prior to the current proliferation of Irish bars and bars with perfectly Irish-sounding names. Out-of-towners should look sharp for bars

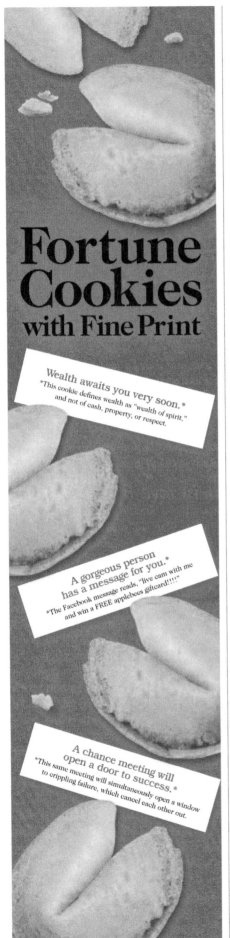

Fortune Cookies
with Fine Print

Wealth awaits you very soon. *
*This cookie defines wealth as "wealth of spirit," and not of cash, property, or respect.

A gorgeous person has a message for you. *
*The Facebook message reads, "live cam with me and win a FREE applebees giftcard!!!!"

A chance meeting will open a door to success. *
*This same meeting will simultaneously open a window to crippling failure, which cancel each other out.

ACTUAL RESULTS MAY VARY

that water down their potions and follow the locals to reputable spots where two drinks make the women sound like Roseanne Barr and the men sound more like Roseanne Barr. Although a nearly respectable neighborhood, tourists should note that in StUMBLES, St. Patrick's Day still is known as "Tuesday, and a school night."

RUMBA *(Residences Under Manhattan Bridge Area)* Characterized by its elevator-free lifestyle and proximity to a true looming architectural wonder, this is the up-and-coming region for those without preferences for a particular type of music. A walk through RUMBA on a warm summer's night is a sternum-thumping smorgasbord of bass notes from car speakers, apartment speakers and speakers in bodegas, restaurants and bars. Music is everywhere, and at a volume sure to dislodge the plaque in your bookie's arteries.

DiaPER *(Diagonal from Prospect Park to the East River)* Not quite Brooklyn Heights, not quite Prospect Park: Mark my words, this is where your more affluent friends will be moving when they finally decide to have that baby. Prepare for plenty of interborough travel if you ever want to see them again, for once they settle into DiaPER, there will be no extracting them from the neighborhood that offers all the dark tree-lined streets of the suburbs without compromising on the prices, dirt and

brunch crowds of the city.

SMIRK *(Secured Mainly In Return for Key Money)* This highly desirable area [*N.B.* SMIRK's borders were disputed by all 17 brokers consulted for this article] is New York City's most fashionable, contains the wittiest and most accomplished residents, and is well-known among the influential few. Home to the best parties and private cultural happenings for the elect, only those in a position to remunerate certain extremely well-connected insiders may live in these elusive large, airy, sunlit apartments which are reputed to inspire torrents of creativity in their passionate and successful owners. If you must, ask around to find SMIRK and discover who lives there and how to get in. But be discreet.

—*M. Sweeney Lawless*

AGENT DOUBLE-0 ZERO.

1) Michael Flynn denies discussing sanctions with the Russians. (2) Flynn says he can't remember what he discussed with the Russians, after he learns that transcripts exist of the phone call. (3) Confronted with direct evidence that he did, in fact, discuss lifting sanctions in exchange for the Russians helping get Trump elected, Flynn makes a break for the White House exit. (4) The left sleeve

of his jacket catches on a door handle. Flynn tugs at it, hard, and it tears away, revealing a sickly, yellowing arm shriveled by disease and disuse. (5) Flynn careens into a tour group of eighth graders. He seizes a young girl, places her in a choke hold with his malformed arm, draws a Makarov pistol and holds it to her head. "Get back," he screams in a terrified falsetto. "So help me God I'll blow her brains out!" (6) Retreating slowly into a corner, Flynn's eyes dart and jump wildly like the eyes of a mad animal. (7) A thin gobbet of spittle hangs from the retired general's lips. (8) "Stay back!" (9) The eighth grade girl kicks upward into Flynn's crotch, causing him to drop the Makarov and double forward in pain. (10) As the girl dashes forward to safety, Secret Service officers quickly close in on him. The former leader of soldiers scrambles for the pistol, but it's too late. "O, woe, I am undone by mine own hand! Is this the end of Michael Flynn?" END ACT II

—*Adrian Bonenberger*

MAKE A WISH.

"Seth, this is President Trump. He's come to see you."

"Oh, wow! Hi!"

"Hello, Seth. I hear you have cancer. Now let me tell you, I know a lot about cancer, and it is really tough. Very brutal and very nasty in so many different ways. So you have to be tough and brutal and nasty, too. Okay, Seth?"

"Yes, sir."

"A lot of people are gonna say you can't do it. But don't listen to them. A lot of people said I couldn't be president. But I won — by a tremendous, tremendous margin by the way. And now I'm president. Which is a very, very prestigious honor that they only give to you if you're like a really smart person."

"Yes, sir."

"But we're gonna straighten it out, Seth, believe me. And the bills and all that. Let me tell you: I know the best bills. Like Bill Belichick. He's a very close friend. I read somewhere that I'm his very best friend and he only smiles when he hears my name. Usually he just scowls, because he has a tremendous IQ and the best thoughts. But he hears 'Trump' and he lights up like you wouldn't believe. I scowl a lot too because I also have the best thoughts, but also because my face weighs 50 pounds. Seth?"

"Yes, sir?"

"Try to stay awake. I have incredible stamina. That's so, so important. It comes from having great genes. My father — do you know who my father was, Seth? He was a great man. He used to take me outside in the wintertime and spray me with the hose and scream, 'Donald, you are a busi-

You will travel to many exotic places in the years to come.*
* This cookie classifies the tropical plants section of Lowe's as "exotic."

A lifetime of happiness is in store for you.*
* Meaning, happiness is in [a] store for you to purchase, but it is out of your price range.

You will be asked to accept a position of great honor.*
* Turn in this fortune to Ethnic Food Products factory in White Plains, NY to be given the exalted position of Fortune Writer. That's right, I'm finally leaving this gig to backpack across Europe for a few years, then I'm going to settle down, get my MBA, and slowly transform into my dad.

You will marry your true love.*
*This cookie is working under the supposition that in the future, it will be legal to marry pizza.

—*Geoffrey Golden*

ness genius, and I love you more than anyone has ever loved anyone in the world, but life is very nasty and unfair and you have to be willing to destroy your opponents — especially the weak little boy who lives in your heart and only comes out late at night." It was beautiful. And that's how you have to be with the cancer, Seth. You have to be very nasty and very tough, like my father was with me and like I am with the boy who lives in my heart. And then maybe someday your cancer will grow up to be president like I did, and its father will love it and it will have the biggest crowds. Well, not the biggest crowds. I have the biggest crowds. Who said cancer's crowds were so big? CNN? FAKE MEDIA. Did you see my crowds, Seth?"

"I'm blind."

"They were the best crowds. Everyone was saying that. They were a hundred, maybe a million times bigger than your cancer's crowds. Tremendous. And my crowds were screaming like the CIA screamed when I gave that speech in front of their very famous hero wall that was probably the greatest speech anyone has ever given, except when my father enters my dreams with his hose and screams at me about my heart-boy. The CIA was very strong on Trump, let me tell you. Very, very special people. You should have come. Actually, you did come. Because everyone came and you are a person. Did you have fun? Seth? Seth?."

"..."

"Do you use Purell? You should. I put it everywhere. Eric loves it even more than I do. He eats it sometimes. He says it helps keep his gills moist. When Eric's gills dry out, he can be a really not very nice person, especially when he enters my dreams and says I look like a Nerf football that got left out in the yard all winter. Sometimes I think he's trying to destroy me because we gave so many of his chromosomes to Ivanka, but let me tell you, it worked, bigly. She is a total knockout. Seth? Seth? I had a special lead-lined bathrobe made to keep Eric out of my dreams at night, but he keeps getting in there, he and my father and the ISIS man and the little boy who lives in my heart. And they tell me very interesting things. Seth? Seth? Did you know Steve Bannon is nothing but dandruff and secrets? Did you know Don Jr.'s hair is just black skin? Did you know stairs are made of germs? Seth, is Eric a *ghost*?"

"Mr. President, this boy has died."

"Wow, look at all the people in here! Another crowd for Trump! They can't stay away. These are very smart doctors. Seth? Seth? You need to work on your stamina. Stamina is so, so important. I have incredible stamina. It comes from having great genes. That's why I never get sick. But you know who's really sick? Rosie. Did you know she said I couldn't be president and have the best crowds, Seth? But I showed her, didn't I? Didn't I, Seth? Didn't I?"

—*Joe Keohane*

ANOTHER WISH.
"I want my keyboard to allow me to Alt-Right-Delete."

—*Paul Lander* B

"Who better to tell the story of the legendary *New Yorker* cartoonist Peter Arno than another legendary *New Yorker* cartoonist Michael Maslin? And what a delight to discover that Maslin's gift for writing equals his talent for drawing. From start to finish, this is book is masterful and unforgettable."

—ANDY BOROWITZ, *New York Times* bestselling author and *New Yorker* columnist

BY JACK HANDEY

WHERE MY CAMPAIGN WENT WRONG

Funny thing: Nate Silver had Jack winning

RON BARRETT

I should have focused more on the issues instead of how the word "focused" is spelled.

I tried to kiss a baby while it was nursing.

I should not have chosen to debate a crazy homeless man instead of my opponent. I thought he would be easy. But the homeless man struck a nerve with his rant: "You know who controls the world?! Budweiser! Budweiser controls the world!"

When I tried to counter with some incoherent babbling, I was accused of plagiarism.

When I made an offhand comment about "some bozo," I lost the clown vote.

At the next debate — this time with my opponent — the question was, "What is the most powerful force in the world?" I started to say atom bombs, but my opponent said "Love," and it got big applause. At the last second, I changed my answer to "*consensual* love," but it got no response. I should have stuck with atom bombs.

Whenever I practiced my speech in the mirror, I accidentally hypnotized myself.

When I announced my running mate, he told the press he was, in fact, not my running mate. Thanks, Dalai Lama.

The assassination attempt did not get me sympathy. When a reporter asked me a smart-alecky question, and I jumped from the stage and tried to assassinate him, I think it set me back.

A big mistake was tiptoeing around all the time, as a joke, which no one got.

So was pointing and laughing at the coffin of my opponent's father. And explaining later that I was drunk didn't help.

At my nomination I was startled by the falling balloons and hid under some chairs.

My standard speech, "Eventually We're All Going to Die," was not a crowd pleaser.

In my campaign literature, somehow, every illustration of a woman showed her holding a rolling pin.

I accused my opponent of inflicting stupid malarkey on us, not realizing that his son is named Malarkey. The boy is struggling in school.

Even though I was in a hurry I should not have been eating a sandwich when I met the pope.

I vowed that, once in office, I would make no other vows.

Calling my opponent a liar and then accidentally catching my pants on fire.

While speaking before a large crowd I was struck with stage fright. I remembered the old trick of imagining everyone in the audience was nude, which I did. But then I started masturbating.

I should have criticized my opponent for not liking me. **B**

JACK HANDEY

is best-known for his "Deep Thoughts." A contributor to **The New Yorker** *and many other publications, he recently self-published* **Squeaky Poems: Rhymes About My Rat.**

BY BEN ORLIN

TALES OF THE GIRL WHO NOBODY REALLY LIKED

BOB GROSSMAN

JACK AND THE BEANSTALK

Jack came scrambling down the beanstalk, his arms full of treasure and his face full of panic. The giant bellowed down, "You rotten thief! You scoundrel! I'll eat you up and spit out the bones!"

Hillary Clinton sighed, rolled up her sleeves and began climbing.

She returned several hours later with a draft of an agreement. "You're going to repatriate the goose and half of the gold coins," she told Jack. "The harp will be licensed to you on an annual basis, renewal subject to negotiation. The good news is that you won't be eaten."

"What about my cow?" said Jack. "I want my cow back from that bean guy."

HANSEL AND GRETEL

"Let's leave a trail of breadcrumbs so we can find our way back!" said Gretel.

"Or," said Hillary Clinton, "you could instead snap twigs along the path. Such a marking system would be less conspicuous, more durable and would conserve food resources."

Hansel rolled his eyes and began to crumble the bread into tiny pieces.

LITTLE RED RIDING HOOD

"But Grandmother!" cried Little Red. "What big eyes you have!"

"I realize this must be difficult for you to hear, Ms. Riding Hood, but this is not your grandmother," said Hillary Clinton. "This is a wolf in a frock."

Grandmother growled.

"You're quite right, Grandmother," said Little Red, narrowing her eyes. "I don't trust her either."

CINDERELLA

"Never fear," said the fairy godmother, with a gleam in her eye. "I can turn those rags into a beautiful ball gown! But be careful: The spell will expire at the stroke of midnight."

"This strikes me as a Band-Aid solution," said Hillary Clinton. "Cinderella, I believe your stepmother is acting in violation of child labor laws. I'd like to introduce you to a social worker and begin getting you the help you need."

Cinderella squealed with delight. "You mean a *real* ball gown?!"

THE EMPEROR'S NEW CLOTHES

"Why, the emperor's new wardrobe is simply marvelous!" someone cried.

"Yeah," replied another, "unlike Hillary Clinton over there. Enough with the pantsuits, lady!"

"But the emperor is naked," said Hillary Clinton.

"Okay, maybe his wardrobe isn't *great*," said a townsperson, "but don't overstate your case."

THE THREE LITTLE PIGS

Hillary Clinton came upon a little pig building a house of wood. "I'm sorry," she said, "but your construction project violates several state and city ordinances."

The pig glared.

"Building codes are for your own protection," she said. "This structure is manifestly unsound."

"Oh, *I* see how it is," said the pig. "I'm the big criminal, and meanwhile my brother is allowed to build his house out of *straw*?!"

Hillary Clinton blinked. "I wasn't aware of that. No, that's also illegal."

With their houses condemned, the two pigs moved in with their elder brother. The living quarters were cramped at best.

"How did they even find out about my house?" asked the straw-house pig. "I was so careful."

"It's that stupid Hillary Clinton!" shouted the wood-house pig. "Our lives would be so much better if we'd never met her!"

"I know," his brother said. "She's the *worst*." **B**

BEN ORLIN *is, surprisingly, a math teacher; and even more surprisingly, a Deputy Editor of* **Bystander**. *He has appeared in* **The Atlantic**, **Slate**, **The Los Angeles Times** *and elsewhere. He lives in Manchester, England.*

BY JOE VEIX

THE MORNING ROUTINES OF HIGHLY SUCCESSFUL PEOPLE

It's no secret that the world's top earners are better than all of us, because they have the most money. Another thing they all have in common is a healthy morning routine. It's worth wondering: How do they *carpe* their *diems*? I talked with all of the big-time money boys to find out!

MARK ZUCKERBERG

Like every real human, I begin each day by swallowing a single egg. After absorbing the sufficient nutrients, I spread petroleum jelly over my entire body, so that my epidural layer does not become chapped by this planet's harsh atmosphere. Then I engage in a number of normal-man tasks, such as breathing oxygen, blinking every 6.2 seconds and conversing with friend.

MARISSA MAYER

Right away, I unlock my phone and start firing people. After I eat breakfast, I fire my assistant, then drop my kids off at school. As I walk through the halls, I fire all of their teachers.

When I get to the office, that's when the real firing begins. I start with heads of various departments, and work my way down. I call their husbands and wives and fire them, too. If they're single, I fire their pets. I fire anything that crosses my path: janitors (fired), decorative ferns (fired), my assistant (rehired and fired).

Once I've eliminated thousands of jobs, I head home and prepare dinner for my family, so that we have something to eat while I fire them.

BILL GATES

I usually sleep in pretty late. After I answer a few emails, I'll spend a couple hours squeezing my handgrips. Now that I'm no longer bogged down with the day-to-day of running Microsoft, I can focus on what I truly love: handshakes.

It's why I got into business in the first place. To me, it's not a simple greeting, or about closing a deal. It's a visceral experience—the firm grip, the lavender smell of fresh lotion on soft skin. The fact is, I get a sexual thrill from taking another man's hand and squeezing it.

You have very nice hands.

PETER THIEL

The sun wakes me at dawn here on Xanadu, my massive floating city of the sea. This waterworld is unsullied by government intervention and trivial social attachments like friends or family. I don't need anyone. It's just me and the fresh salt air, a libertarian hero, living only by his wits and gritty self-determination.

Hey, where are you going? Please don't leave. I'm so lonely.

RICHARD BRANSON

The early bird gets the worm, as the popular saying goes. That's why I always wake up at 5a.m. and consume an 11-pound bucket of live bait.

ELON MUSK

I start working immediately. I have no time to squander on petty human distractions, like "eating breakfast" or "drinking coffee" or "bowel movements." That's right, I've invented a new system in which I no longer defecate. All of my waste is absorbed into my bloodstream and then excreted out of my pores as a fetid steam. Objectively, I smell quite bad.

I spend the extra time I would have wasted on the toilet preparing to launch my body into space, so that one day I can live beneath the dusty soil of Mars like a terrible Mole King.

TIM COOK

I don't have mornings, per se, because I rarely sleep. Often, late at night, the ghosts of workers who died in Apple factories visit me. I steal their ideas.

ELIZABETH HOLMES

Have you ever hunted a man?

Yes, you heard me. I'm speaking of the most dangerous game of all, hunting a human being for sport. Shooting an arrow, clean and true, straight through their heart. Taking their throat within your maw and ripping apart all the loose meat. Tasting the life as it spills out of them. Rushing through the fields beneath the moaning blood moon looking for another victim, because the hunger—that awful hunger!—won't cease.

Sorry, what was the question?

[Shortly after filing this piece, its author went missing. He was last seen interviewing Elizabeth Holmes in Palo Alto. If you have any information, please call the FBI's anonymous tip line at 1-855-835-5324. His family just wants closure.] B

JOE VEIX *(@joeveix) is the culture editor at* **Newsweek,** *and has written for* **The New Yorker, Vice** *and* **Playboy.** *He lives on a big hill in Oakland.*

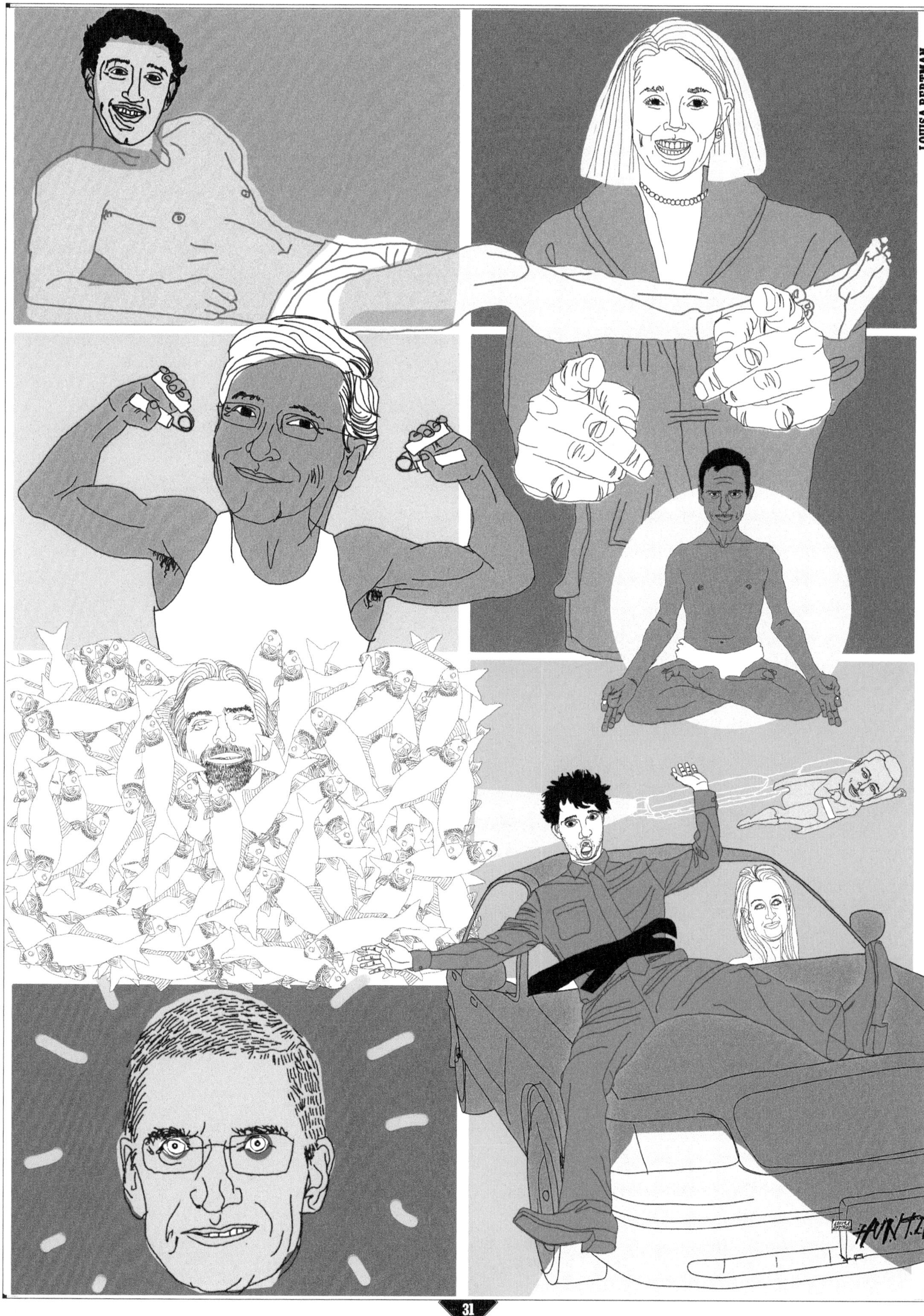

LOUISA BERTMAN

BY ROB KUTNER

@HANKYTHO69

Live-tweeting Walden

I went to the woods to live deliberately. #ButMostlyBecauseIGotDumped

I wanted to live deep and suck out all the marrow of life. #Note:LifeMarrow=ZeroCalories

I lived alone…in a house which I had built myself, on the shore of Walden Pond…and earned my living by the labor of my hands only. #NBD

I came to occupy my house on the 4th of July. #IndependenceDay #GetIt? #NailedIt

I laid the foundation of a chimney… bringing two cartloads of stones up the hill in my arms. #WelcomeToTheGunShowLadies

This was an airy and unplastered cabin…where a goddess might trail her garments. #AndBelieveMeManyDid

The necessaries of life for man…may be distributed under the several heads of Food, Shelter, Clothing, and Fuel. #AndWiFi

I could sometimes eat a fried rat with a good relish, if it were necessary. #NomNomNom

I will only hint at some of the enterprises which I have cherished. #RhymesWith"Rasturbation"

I found that, by working about six weeks in a year, I could meet all the expenses of living. #ImAStateLegislator

For many years I was self-appointed inspector of snow-storms and rain-storms, and did my duty faithfully. #YesItsARealJobDAD

I say, beware of all enterprises that require new clothes. #ApplyingToBeHipsterBarista

Most men live lives of quiet desperation. #TheyAreInSales

There is no odor so bad as that which arises from goodness tainted. #AndMyHomemade"Toilet"

"Carpenter" is but another name for "coffin-maker." #ThoreauSnaps

The better part of the man is soon plowed into the soil for compost. #ThoreauSnaps

Men have become the tools of their tools. #WorkInProgress #DontJudge

Man thus not only works for the animal within him, but he works for the animal without him. #JustDiscoveredGanjaPatch

Sometimes, in a summer morning, having taken my accustomed bath, I sat in my sunny doorway from sunrise till noon, in a revery. #SeeAbove

I did not read books the first summer; I hoed beans. #HosBeforeKnows #SeemedFunnierInMyHead

The wasps came by thousands to my lodge in October. #TheyWereNamedChesterAndMuffy

For a week of even weather, I took exactly the same number of steps, and of the same length, coming and going. #ImFun!

At this season I seldom had a visitor. #GottaCleanThatHomemade"Toilet"

What more can a reasonable man desire…than a sufficient number of ears of green sweet corn boiled, with the addition of salt? #SoooLonely

As long as possible live free and uncommitted. It makes little difference whether you are committed to a farm or jail. #WeddingToast

Be a Columbus to whole new continents and worlds within you. #SlaughterTheIndiansOfYourMind

It is not worth the while to go round the world to count the cats in Zanzibar. #CatPost #Viral

I left the woods for as good a reason as I went there. #LostWiFi

B

ROB KUTNER

writes for Conan, *wrote for* The Daily Show, *and authored the book* Apocalypse How: Turn the End-Times into the Best of Times *and the Howl.fm series* Runaway Brains *(@ApocalypseHow).*

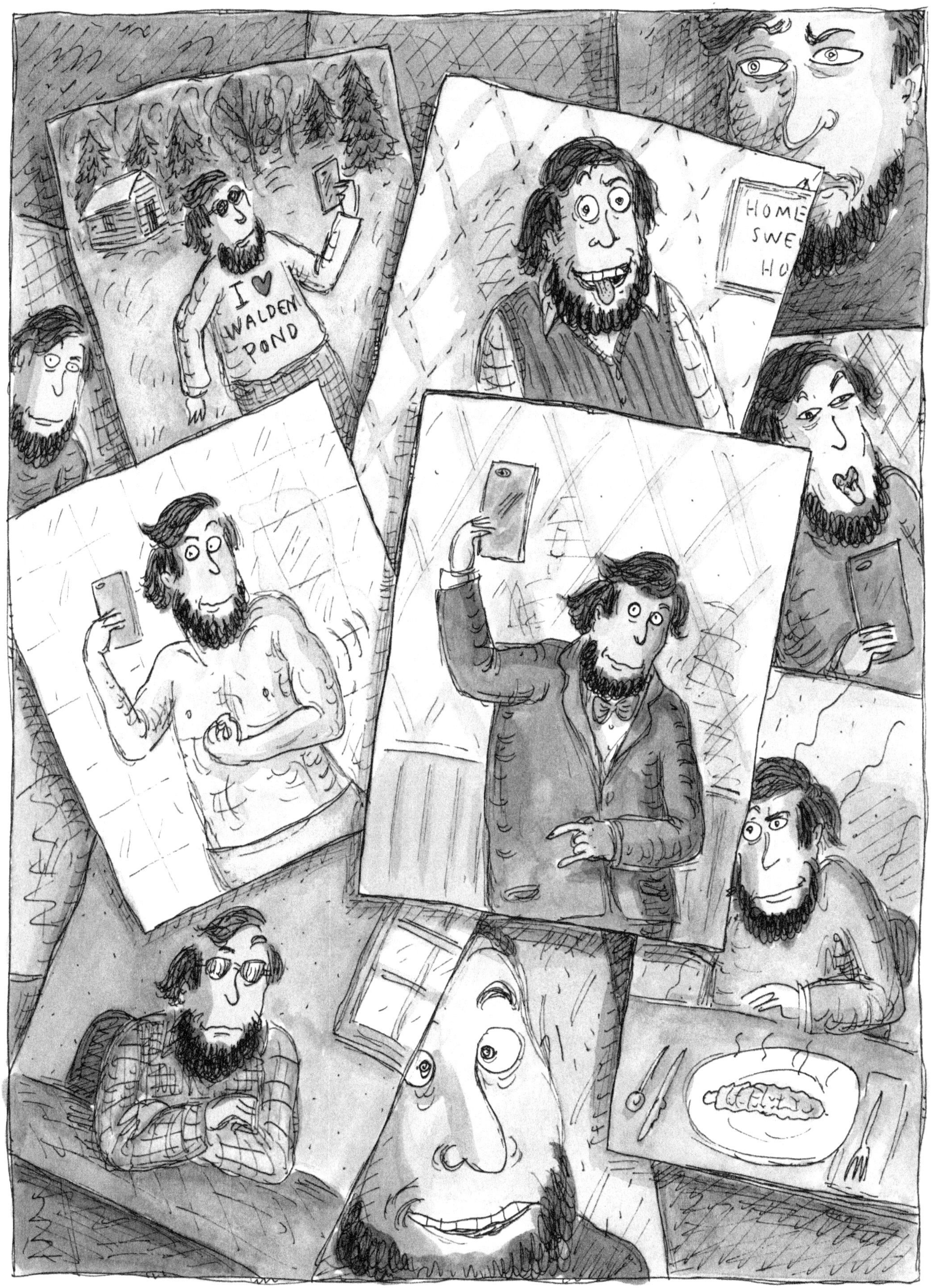
I ♥ WALDEN POND
HOME SWE HO
R. Chast

BY P.S. MUELLER

WEATHER SPACE COMMAND

When the rain in Spain falls mainly on the plain... that's me

I don't actually command weather from up here, but I do tweak it a bit with the help of technology I don't understand and can't really talk about. My job involves six-month tours of duty on a commercially owned orbital station moving at about 17,000 MPH 200 miles above your corn, soybeans and rice. I manipulate regional weather patterns at the behest of futures traders. My code name is Sky God.

Last week when conditions were right, I had the opportunity to sufficiently nudge monsoonal rains in Asia to assure that certain investments in rice would make a hundred million dollars with far less speculation than had been required until fairly recently. A week earlier, I brought rain to a million acres of wheat in Kansas by following a computer model sent up by our people in Chicago.

This type of work isn't nearly as fun as you would think, especially if you're paired with Earl. He chews tobacco and sneezes frequently, always a lethal combination in zero G. Add that to his compulsive use of talcum powder and it makes for a really long shift. Plus, Earl talks about tits, constantly. Honest to God, if I point out a devastating typhoon approaching, say, Sumatra, Earl can pull the subject around to his annoyance over cloud cover obscuring his view of what he calls "Geographic mams" and stay worked up about it for hours. By the way, we can see everybody's tits from up here, which probably explains why Earl blew a carefully planned crop failure in France last week during my sleep period.

We are in the same orbit as Wally Baumgartner, who floated free of the Space Shuttle back in the '90s. You didn't hear about it in the news then, because Wally was an unlisted passenger, sent up by the Clinton people to keep an eye on suspected Afghan terrorists. The story goes that Wally had pestered the crew for weeks to go along on a space walk, and when he finally got his chance, something went wrong with his tether and he floated away. He wasn't officially onboard, so nothing was done to retrieve him, and ever since then, we pass the guy every three and a half days. A couple of years ago, the Russians managed to snag him just long enough to slip on a giant foam rubber "We're No. 37" glove onto his right hand, supposedly to make him easier to see and avoid. I don't think so.

A few days ago, Earl and I had a long teleconference with the people in Chicago about a super hush-hush project involving Honduras. They wanted us to build a freak weather system in Eastern Siberia and run it all the way down the Pacific and across the mainland to freeze every last banana from Tela to Puerto Castilla. I told them that in my humble opinion the operation was too ambitious and could be seen in some quarters as overly greedy, but I was dismissed out of hand. "You just run the programs," they told me. "We know what we're doing." Then one of the older execs leaned into the camera and mentioned something about Wally looking especially lonely these days.

So a couple of days later, we froze the crop. The cold front we dropped on Honduras was unprecedented, but the Chicago guys aroused no suspicion at all with their hinky trades, and the whole disaster was blamed on a disturbance in the upper atmosphere caused by global warming. However, the computer models only took the frozen air that far, not bothering to follow through on what might happen after the air mass headed into the Caribbean, which it did. By the next morning, clouds covered the entire Gulf of Mexico and began spreading across the Atlantic, quickly obscuring our view and moving at roughly the same speed as our module.

Before a week had passed, the entire planet was enveloped in a solid white envelope of thick stratus clouds, and we could see nothing below us. Lightning flickered intermittently everywhere down there, and we heard nothing more from Chicago.

Now we have no idea what to do. The guys over at the International Space Station don't know anything either. There is enough food to last us the better part of a year, and we could try to wait things out. But then again, if we decide to head home on the emergency return vehicle, what if we land in the sea and no one knows we're back? At least Earl has stopped talking about tits. **B**

P.S. MUELLER *is a cartoonist, writer, voice actor and dental patient. But you probably know him best as "Doyle Redmond," newsreader for* **The Onion Radio News.**

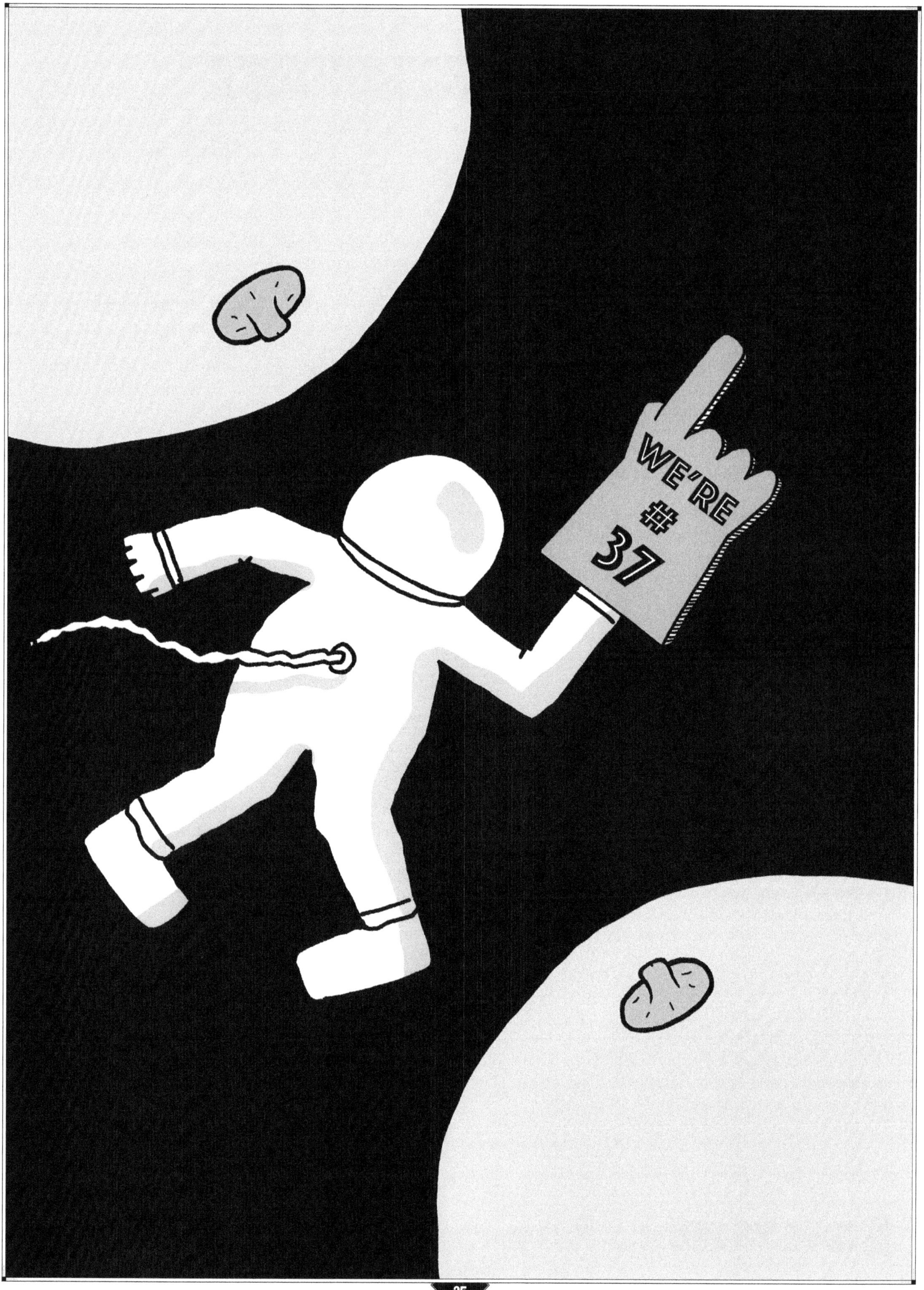
WE'RE
#
37

P.S. MUELLER

BY STEVE YOUNG

WELCOME TO METROHURT

A Guide for Patients in Transport!

Welcome aboard MetroHurt Ambulance! Sorry you're not well, but we hope your ride with us today is as pleasant as your serious injury or illness permits! We ask that those of you who are conscious take a moment to review these guidelines. Failure to comply may result in your ejection from the ambulance.

You must complete the health insurance questionnaire prior to transport. Depending on the quality of your health insurance, you may receive medical supplies classified as "sterile," "like new" or "classic."

It is the patient's responsibility to provide a gurney. If you do not have a gurney, $524.99 will be added to your bill following a time-consuming stop at a medical supply store.

Smoking is not permitted in the ambulance. The only exception is if you were rescued from a fire, and your clothing or flesh is still smoldering. Please extinguish yourself as soon as possible!

Do not direct the driver. Be assured that you will be transported via the fastest route to the nearest hospital, unless your condition is stable and the crew needs to do errands or get the ambulance washed.

Do not use the defibrillator paddles to make pressed sandwiches. Only certified EMT personnel may use the defibrillator equipment for medical or sandwich purposes.

While we understand that you may be in agonizing pain, please restrict yourself to low moans and sighs. Screams and yells will upset Sepsis, the ambulance cat.

Do not take MetroHurt Ambulance if you are allergic to cats.

Wifi is available during transport for a nominal fee. On your device, select the network MetroHurtGuest and use the password "BleedOut." Your connection may be slow if the paramedics are consulting WebMD.

Do not open the pizza boxes. MetroHurt Ambulance also delivers Pete's Famous Pizza, and customers understandably do not want their pizza touched by sick people.

The ambulance may stop to pick up other patients if you selected MetroHurt Pool rather than MetroHurt X. Please make room. If you must cough, cough into your elbow or the elbow of a fellow patient.

The siren will be activated only if your hospital transport coincides with an urgent pizza delivery. Do not request non-pizza siren usage.

Bites and/or scratches inflicted by Sepsis the cat during her noise-induced panics are the sole responsibility of the patient. If these injuries are serious, you may wish to call a different ambulance.

If you are physically and mentally able, you may be asked to drive the ambulance so the driver can nap. Follow all traffic rules and regulations!

Prior to disembarking from the MetroHurt ambulance, you must pay for any liquor or other goods ordered from the SickMall catalog.

If things go badly during your transport and you find yourself in a long tunnel with light at the end, you'll notice that in addition to the beckoning forms of deceased loved ones, you will see a MetroHurt representative asking you to sign a liability waiver. Sign this document.

Assuming you survive, a positive Yelp review would be greatly appreciated!

Thanks for riding with us today, best of luck with your medical issue, and we hope to see you again soon in a MetroHurt Ambulance! **B**

STEVE YOUNG *(@pantssteve) is a veteran* Letterman *writer who's also written for* The Simpsons. *He recently worked on NBC's* Maya & Marty *variety show and is teaching a course at NYU's Tisch School.*

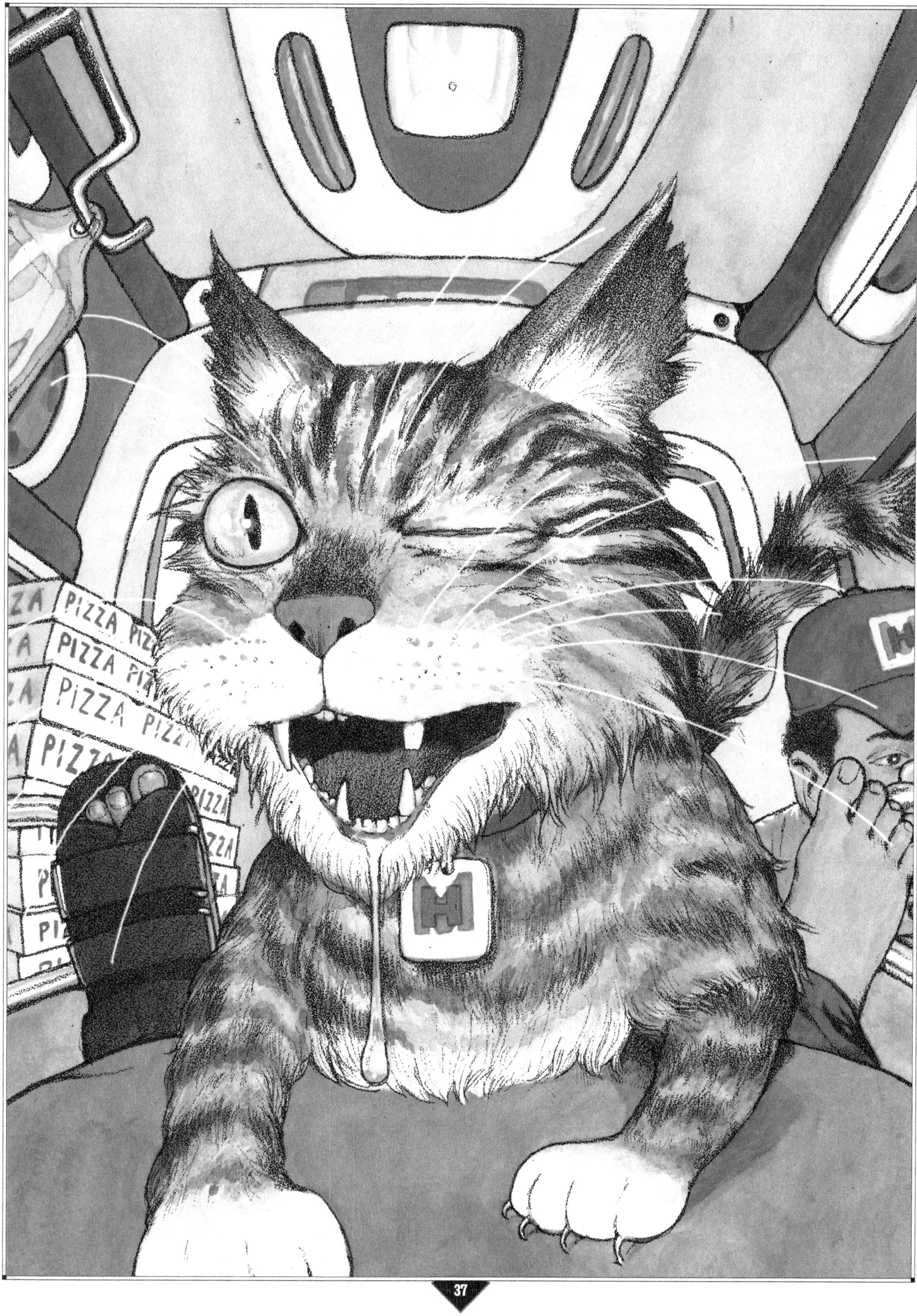
PIZZA
PIZZA
PIZZA
PIZZA
H
H

DAVID CHELSEA

BY LARRY DOYLE

KEEP ON CRUISIN'

Greetings from "The Unhappiest Place Under Earth"

Disney riverboats could be entirely new canvases in which to let the Walt Disney Imagineers unleash their creativity on, integrating storytelling into the very nuts and bolts, decor and fixtures, setting the scene for adventures to come."— Do More Disney River Cruises Foreshadow Dedicated Cruise Line?, *Travel Pulse.*

Good morning! Or evening! Whichever, let's make the best of it!

Welcome once again to Adventures by Disney's Royal Subterranean River Cruise. I'm Larry, your cruise director, bringing you the latest Lowdown from Down Under for the next Tuesday or possibly Wednesday of Eternity.

REMINDER

Please remember to take the *danakes* from your eyes when you awake and keep them safe. You will need these coins at the end of the cruise. You don't have pockets so you will have to hold on to them. As they will sear your flesh, our ship's physician, Doc, recommends that you don't carry them anywhere but in your hands.

TODAY'S WEATHER

You're way ahead of me: It's going to be another scorcher! Pray for a break in the writhing by late afternoon when there's a chance of scattered blood showers. Tonight will be nippy beyond imagining, so please remember to wear your hairshirt!

REMINDER

Please remember this is a nonsmoking cruise. If you must smoke, please drag your smoldering remains up to the Princess Ariel lido deck and hurl yourself into one of our three Olympic-sized smoking pits.

NEWS FROM THE SURFACE

Your wife has married your neighbor Brian, the guy who shot you in the throat at that tailgate party. (It was ruled accidental!) The deliriously happy newlyweds report that your little Molly calls him "Daddy Bee." Isn't that adorable?

Also, that boy who copied off your civics test and then ratted you out for cheating is now the president of the United States.

Oh, and they cured your kind of cancer. If only you hadn't been shot in the throat by Brian, your wife's beloved husband… well, there's no point in dwelling on that now!

But do dwell on it.

REMINDER

Please remember you are required to spend at least one hour head-down in the Goofy Poop Deck.

TODAY'S ADVENTURES

Let's see what our Dark Imagineers have brewed up for you today!

• You were likely visited in the night by lovable Sully, irascible Randall, or a succubus. Well, this morning from 4 to 5 AM you can meet them for a Monster's Breakfast in the Bilge Room. Grab a selfie and get your hearts or genitals back!

• Scrooge McDuck will be threaded through the eye of a needle at 11 AM and 1, 3 and 5 PM.

• Today's Offshore Adventure is once again a jaunt to Disney Underworld, where you will wait in line until it's time to return to the ship.

• And of course, every endless day ends with our Disney Parade of the Damned, whipped endlessly by our Seven Demons: Beezle, Bubby, Agony, Bloodthirsty, Insaney, Floggy and Bashful. Survive the flailing and stick around for our Spectacular Cleansing Fire Display.

REMINDER

Parents who wish to gamble and fornicate may dump their tykes at Cruella's Puppy Mill. Please remember to pick them up before feeding time. And also please remember these are not your real spawn. They are memories of the children you once had but who have grown and never talk of you.

MOVIE NIGHT!

We will be screening Disney-Miramax's *Duplex* (2003), an alleged comedy starring Ben Stiller and Drew Barrymore. It's the story of a young couple who try to kill a sweet old lady for her New York apartment — and you thought *you* were bad! Check the seats around you to see if you can spot the immortal soul of director Danny DeVito, awaiting the arrival of his earthly vessel. And in the front row

(continued on p. 95)

LARRY DOYLE *(@thelarrydoyle) is a frequent contributor to* **The New Yorker.** *His first novel,* **I Love You, Beth Cooper,** *won the 2008 Thurber Prize for American Humor and was made into a movie.*

JOE OESTERLE

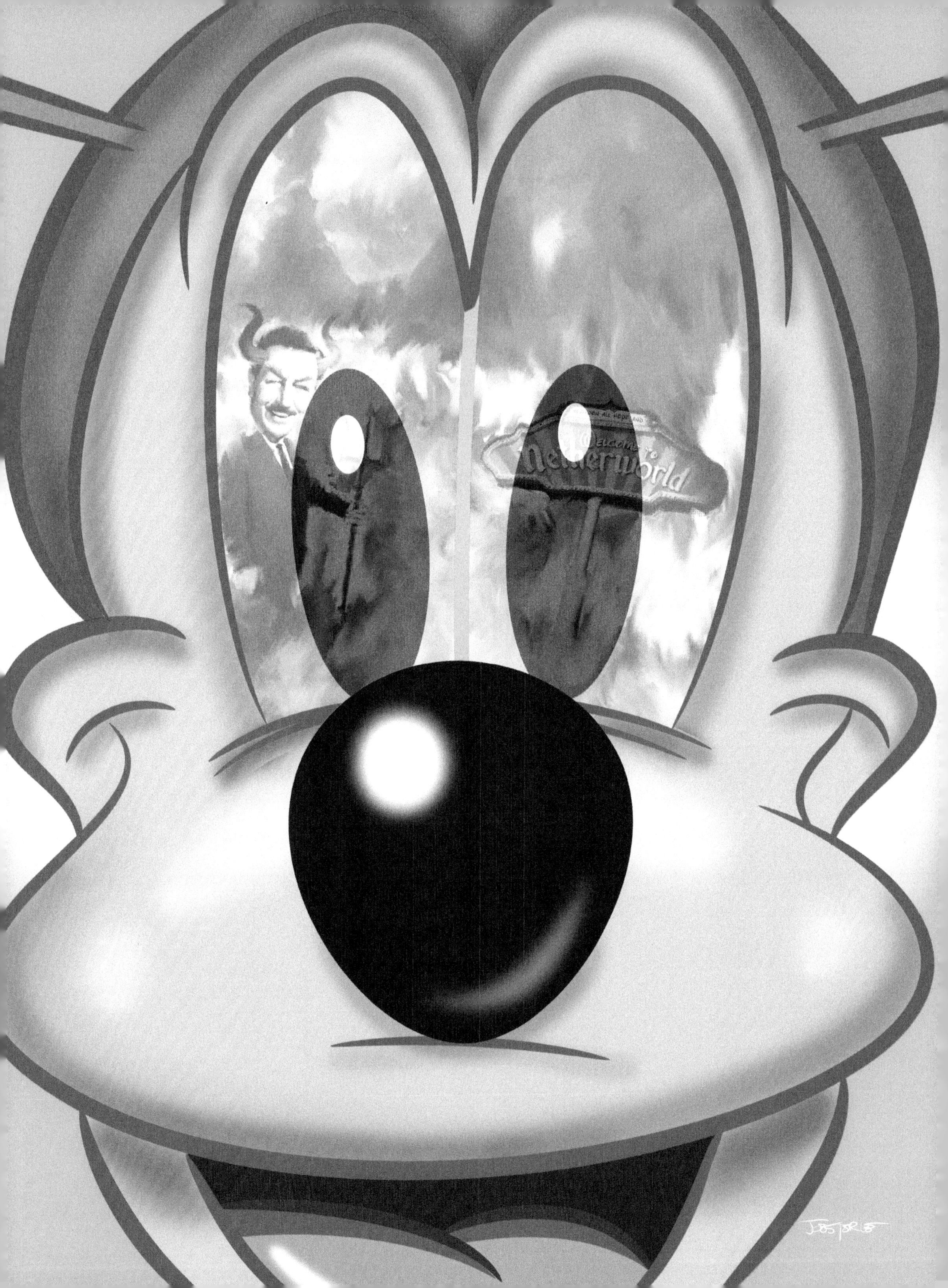
Welcome to Netherworld

THE DREW FRIEDMAN
LIBRARY FROM FANTAGRAPHICS BOOKS

"I'm grateful to Drew Friedman for every new piece in his vast, riveting panorama of the jacked-up, hellbent american spectacle: comic and horrific, loving and appalled, obsessive and devil-may-care, brilliant and vulgar, familiar and uncanny. He's our own William Hogarth and Thomas Rowlandson and George Grosz all wrapped into one."
— *Kurt Anderson, host of NPR's Studio 360*

"Drew Friedman isn't just a brilliant artist. He makes you smell the stale cigarettes and cold brisket and you say, thank you for the pleasure." — *Sarah Silverman*

"I love Drew friedman. He's my favorite artist."
— *Howard Stern*

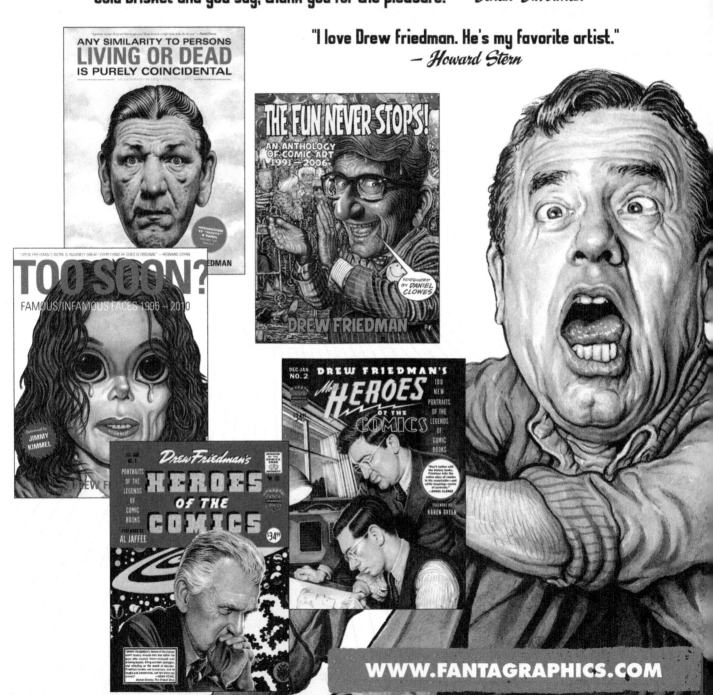

The TRAGEDY of MERMEN

YOUR BACK'S REALLY GETTING RED!

WHAT ARE THE FISH DOING?

JUST SWIMMING THIS WAY AND THAT WITH STUPID LOOKS ON THEIR

A LITTLE COLD AT FIRST BUT YOU GET USED TO IT.

CATCH IT THIS TIME.

JUST TOSS THE COCONUT.

HOW'S THE WATER?

I'LL TRADE THESE SHELLS FOR IT.

THEIR LIFE WAS MOSTLY HABIT...

THEY BELIEVED THE CLOUDS WERE FIXED IN THE SKY AND THEIR ISLAND WAS TRAVELING THROUGH THE WATER...

A SHIFT! WE'RE GOING SIDEWAYS AGAIN! QUICK! TO THE OTHER BEACH!

IT WAS THEIR DUTY TO ALWAYS FACE THE DIRECTION IN WHICH THEY WERE HEADED. THERE THE FUTURE WOULD APPEAR...

DID SOMEONE REMEMBER TO BRING THE COCONUTS?

DO YOU THINK WE'LL ARRIVE AT OUR DESTINY TODAY?

COULD BE. WE SEEM TO BE MOVING PRETTY FAST.

BUT LIFE IS LONG AND EVERY NOW AND THEN A DISTURBING FEELING WOULD COME TO EACH OF THEM - A FEELING THAT SOMETHING WAS EITHER MISSING OR INUTTERABLY WRONG!

I'LL TRADE YOU THIS ONE FOR THEM.

TAKE THEM ALL! I DON'T CARE! SHELLS ARE ALL OVER THE BEACH. WHAT DIFFERENCE DOES IT MAKE?

THEY NEVER DISCUSSED THE "FEELING" BUT THEY COULD SPOT IT IN ONE ANOTHER...

HE'S BEEN LIKE THAT FOR DAYS!

THEN, ONE DAY A GREAT CHANGE CAME! I'VE BEEN WATCHING THE WATER AND THE STICKS. I SAY WE'RE NOT GOING FORWARD INTO THE FUTURE — WE ARE GOING UP AND DOWN IN THE PRESENT!

THAT'S ONE FOR THE FISH!

BUT THE MORE THEY TRIED NOT TO THINK ABOUT IT, THE MORE TROUBLED THEY FELT. UNTIL ONE FINALLY VOICED THEIR DEEPEST FEAR.

IN ALL THIS TIME WE HAVEN'T MOVED!!

AFTER A LONG, HEATED DEBATE, THEY DECIDED TO GO IN SEARCH OF THEIR DESTINY.

SEE ANYTHING?

YEAH! MY HANDS ARE GETTING REAL WRINKLED!

THEIR SEARCH CONTINUED FOR MANY DAYS UNTIL FINALLY...

LOOK! OUR DESTINY!

QUICK! WE MUST SING SOMETHING!

LIKE WHAT?

WHAT **ARE** THEY?

MEANWHILE...

YOO HOO!

NICE BEACH!

HELLO!

I WONDER WHO LIVES HERE?

LOOK! COCONUTS!

I HATE COCONUTS! IT'S LIKE EATING HAIR!

THESE ARE EVIL WATERS!

WILL YOU LOOK AT THIS!?

LET GO OF MY **LEG**!

NO! THEY MAY BE POSSESSED OF AN IMMORTAL SOUL!

I'LL TRADE MY SHELLS FOR THIS! YIIII!!

DROP IT!!

GROW BREASTS AND SHAVE!

EVENTUALLY, THEY DECIDED THEY HAD **TWO** DESTINIES: THAT ONE, AND A BETTER ONE. AND THOUGH THEY MAY NOT BE TRAVELING TOWARDS THE **BETTER ONE**, IT COULD BE BLOWING TOWARDS THEM. SO THINGS RETURNED TO THE WAY THEY HAD BEEN —EXCEPT EVERY NOW AND THEN, THEY'D BE UNPLEASANT TO THE FISH.

NEXT TIME: WHAT CAME FIRST: THE MERBABY OR THE EGG?

B

Paul Bunyan: The Later Years

Now, I've spun you young 'uns some wild yarns about mighty Paul Bunyan before, tales so tall you can't see the top of the CliffsNotes, but I don't recall as I've ever told you about his 50-plus years. It's been many a winter now since the time of Paul Bunyan, you realize, and some folks don't believe that any of Paul's adventures really happened. But those folks... eh, it's just a whole bunch of things with those folks.

Where do Paul's autumn years start? Well, I suppose things started going downhill when he pulled that back muscle chopping down a big old sycamore forest that stretched all the way across Kansas... the Great Plains, they call it now, of course. Y'see, Paul was out there swinging his mighty two-edger back and a-forth, when suddenly he felt a pain shooting up his back, like a herd of buffalo was stampeding up his fifth through ninth vertebrae. Well, he let out a groan that made Missouri think rain must be coming, and the logging camp called for the six finest doctors in the Midwest to come check him out. They gave Paul a complete physical and told him that nothing major was wrong, but he should take it easy in the future, and do more stretching — I know you don't fully believe me, but that's exactly how it went, see.

Then there was the fall of 1898, and Paul's big cancer scare. See, Paul had this mole the size of a pie plate on his leg, but one day when he was taking his morning bath in Lake Huron, he looked down and saw that it was bigger'n a wagon wheel. Well, it took a doctor and three lumberjacks an hour using shovels and saws to remove that mole, and after three worrisome days the biopsy came back negative, but the whole thing was still enough to put the fear of the Maker into Paul. That plus his heart scare the followin' winter made him change his eating habits, and they say three pig farmers went to the poorhouse just from Paul giving up bacon, and he bankrupted half the barley industry by cutting down on beer.

Now, it was just about this time that Paul started getting up two or three times a night to urinate. This was bad not just for the lumber camp, since one of Paul's footsteps sounded like a thunderclap, but it's also a common warning sign of diabetes, which would be bad news indeed. Well, Paul's doctor knew that he'd have to check out the waterworks to see for sure, and do you know, it took 12 lumberjacks all day to hollow out a mighty California Redwood to make a catheter big enough for old Paul Bunyan's urethra, yes it did.

So, long story short, it turned out that it was his prostate. Now some of you kids might have an older relative who's had prostate trouble before, but this was Paul Bunyan, the biggest lumberjack of them all, we're talking about. It took a boxcar full of antibiotics every day just to reduce the symptoms of prostatitis in Paul! They didn't completely cure it, mind ya, but they reduced the flare-ups enough that in the end they decided surgery would be more trouble than it was worth.

Well, right around the time Paul built Babe the Blue Ox's grave, known today as the Blue Ridge Mountains, he started getting winded earlier and earlier in the day, and finally the bosses at the lumber company thought it was high time they retired the old boy. So everyone at the logging camp pitched in for the retirement party, and together they baked a sponge cake as high as Pikes Peak, and Mother Nature herself frosted it. Everyone also chipped in to make a humorous, Paul Bunyan-sized "Old Geezer Survival Kit" including a cane as tall as a telegraph pole and "Can't Get It Up Pills" the size of ponies, and a fine old time was had by all.

So Paul took his pension and bought an apartment in a nice little retirement community down in Tampa. Now housing Paul Bunyan posed a special problem for the management of Sunny Acres, but as luck had it, the local rec center had just closed, and they were able to convert the gymnasium into a Paul-sized apartment, with just a little funding from the Americans with Disabilities Act.

And let me tell you, you would not believe the nice neighbors Paul had! Why, there was Abe Saperstein, a retired shoe salesman who had once sold shoes to the mayor of San Francisco. There was Clarence Gottlieb, who used to run a profitable tool-and-die business. And there was Helen Rickard, who decorated her apartment with little paper flowers she made herself, and that's the God's honest truth I'm telling you. And although retirement was a big change, Paul sure enough adjusted, and soon became one of the complex's best shuffleboard players (holding the cue between his thumb and forefinger), and he kept in shape by walking from Tampa to Oregon and back every morning before breakfast.

(continued)

············ ◆ ············

Tim Harrod *has thought up jokes for* **The Onion, Late Night with Conan O'Brien,** *and the* **Late Show with David Letterman.**

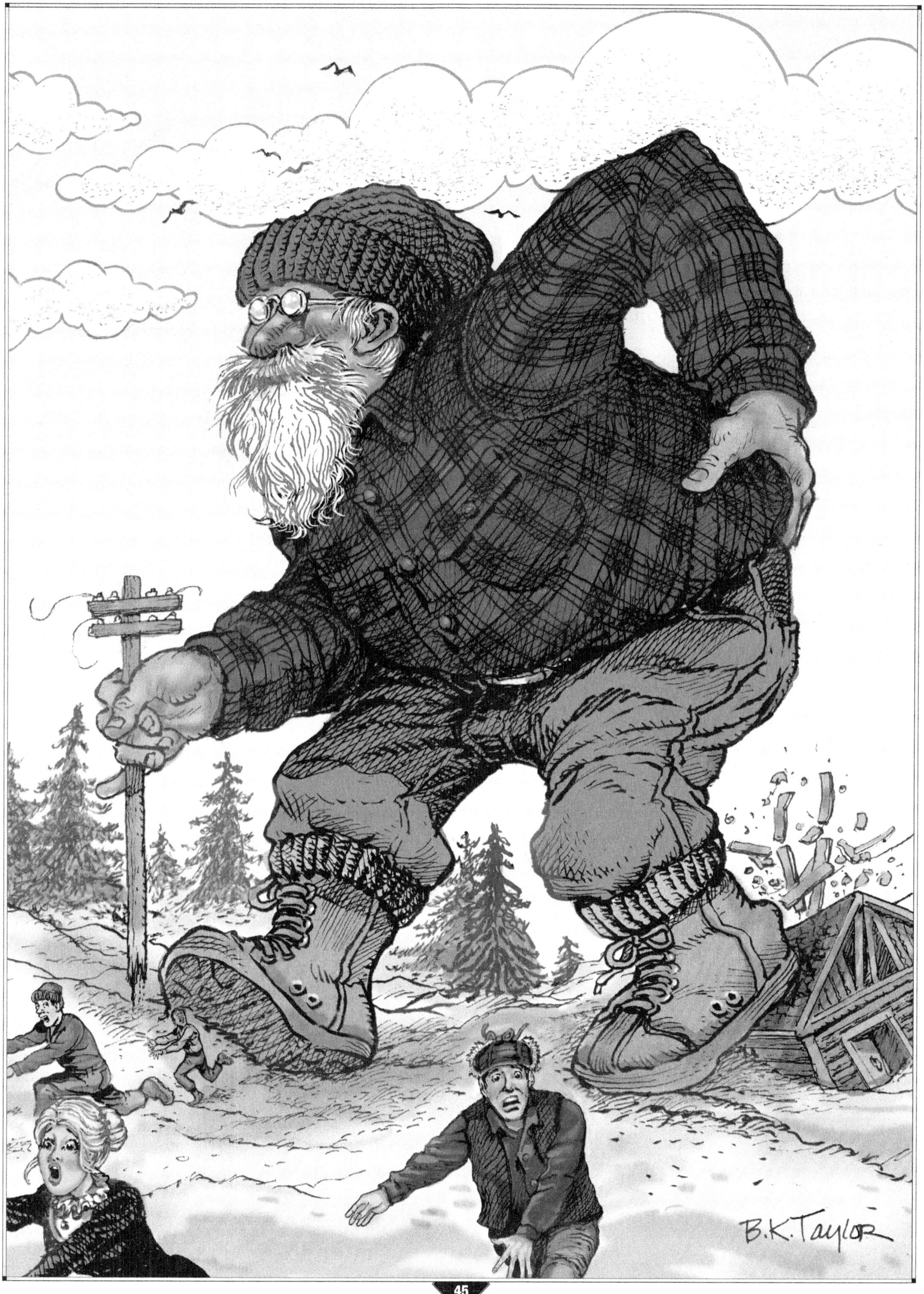
B.K.Taylor

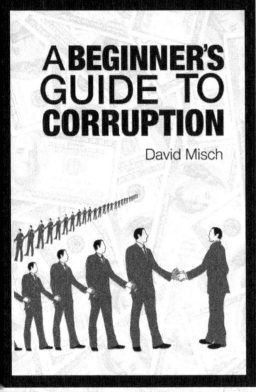
Well, by and by Paul's pension ran out, and the money started getting as tight a Scottish drum, especially since Social Security was only some $200 a month. And one sad, serious day, Paul was reviewing his household finances when he saw a Grand Canyon-sized hole in his budget staring back at him. But Paul was never the quittin' type — he knew right then and there how to plug that hole. He went outside and pulled up two great big lengths of railroad track, and he bent them into the biggest pair of scissors anybody ever saw. And with those mighty scissors in one hand, and the Sunday *Miami Herald* in t'other, Paul set himself to clipping, and clipping, and clipping every coupon in sight. From sunup to sundown, he clipped! He clipped coupons from the Piggly Wiggly circular and *Parade* magazine, he clipped coupons Pillsbury didn't realize they'd even printed, and when it was all over he'd saved so much money that Procter & Gamble owed him three dollars.

Around the time he turned 80, Paul was getting to be as absent-minded as the day is long. Why, he could forget an entire book before he'd finished the foreword, and he'd ask you what time it was before you could look at your watch from the last time he asked. The retirement community was worried about whether this was just the regular onset of age or a more serious neurocognitive disorder, but his spells seemed harmless enough so they let it slide. Until a few months later, when he started waking up at strange times and asking for Spudcake Sam, the old logging camp cook who had, in fact, died eight years before. At that point they brought in a neurologist who confirmed that Paul was suffering Alzheimer's-like symptoms, and that meant it was time to move him to a full-time care facility. So they bundled up Paul in a quilt made of 400 king-size blankets, and it took 12 lumber wagons pulled by ox teams to get him to a nursing home they found that was next to a disused warehouse, which they were able to turn into a little room for Paul.

There aren't a lot of thrilling yarns about Paul's adventures at the home, though he ate a silo full of applesauce every day, and he called his nurse Sheila, which wasn't her name, so that was kind of funny.

And finally, one night nature caught up to even the mighty Paul Bunyan, and they say it gave two hundred angels considerable muscle strain to haul him to his reward. Paul's will provided that he be cremated, and his ashes spread in the mighty Pacific. You might even have heard of it! Today they call it "The Beach."

And you kids who are still listening can bank on that. Come back tomorrow, and I'll tell you the tale of how old Brer Throat tricked Brer Pertussis Bacterium into infecting himself. **B**

"Oh Vlad. You're such a person-half-empty sort of person."

TERRIERS of the FAMOUS

Lester Amis badgers Charles Dickens for a toss of Blackpool Frisbee on the shingle.

Little Eudora riding shotgun on the head of Powderface with Buffalo Bill Cody.

The fetching Jocasta analyses Sigmund Freud's throwing arm with free association.

Tremblement de Terre disrupts the studio of Henri de Toulouse Lautrec.

Barbie Noir sails the Caribbean with Edward Teach on Queen Anne's Revenge.

Really, Really Vladimir enjoys the Nutcracker with his Maestro Tchaikovsky.

············ ◆ ············

Ted Jouflas *is an illustrator/cartoonist whose work has disappeared internationally.*
He is the author of many short stories and two graphic novels, **Scary!** *and* **Filthy**.

Labor Day

Situation: Last summer.
Our pregnant daughter-in-law, Barbara Graber, visited her obstetrician to discuss the impending birth of our grandson.

Dr. Fisher: Everything checks out beautifully, Barbara. In two weeks, you're going to have a healthy baby boy.

Barbara: In two weeks? My due date is September 6th, and that's three weeks from now.

Dr. Fisher: I wanted to talk to you about that. How do you feel about me inducing labor the week before? I'm going skiing and won't be back until the 8th.

Barbara: Skiing in August?

Dr. Fisher: We're going to South America. It's winter there.

Barbara: Well, let me speak to my husband and I'll get back to you.

Heaven. Two weeks later.
God is looking over the list of newborns.

God: Barbara Graber had her baby? She wasn't due for another week.

Assistant: Her doctor moved the date up because he's going skiing in South America. You look mad.

God: Don't I have a say in these things anymore? Who's her doctor?

Assistant: Scott Fisher...

God: Fat guy? Pinky ring? Scratches his back with a fork in fancy restaurants?

Assistant: That's him...

God: He skis?

Assistant: Not very well, but he just bought all new equipment...

God: He can't get away with this. What if I move South America to North America so all the snow melts under his new equipment?

Assistant: Huh...?

God: Or give him a cold sore? One that starts at his lip, goes up his face and then down his back?

Assistant: You could do that?

God: I parted the Red Sea, remember? A cold sore the size of a welcome mat is *kinderspiel* in comparison.

Assistant: I know you have the ability. What I meant was could you morally be that vengeful just because someone exercised free will?

God: That's not free will. Choosing a cable package or deciding if you're going to return the cash with the wallet you found is free will. That's a lot different than determining when a healthy child comes into the world, which is my job and should be discouraged because it's... what's the word I'm looking for?

Assistant: Blasphemous?

God: Worse.

Assistant: Rude?

God: That's it. Rude.

Assistant: You always were a stickler for manners.

Heaven. One week later.
God is looking over the list of dead people.

God: Scott Fisher died? He was supposed to live another 23 years.

Assistant: He committed suicide.

God: Suicide...?

Assistant: According to all reports, he was skiing and when the snow under him melted, he tripped on the grass, broke both legs and when the doctor said he'd never ski again he got so upset he went home and shot himself. For the record, I'm sure his unsightly cold sore did little to lift his spirits.

God: So let me see if I understand this correctly. The same man who screwed me by prematurely bringing a life into this world, screwed me a second time by taking his own life out of this world?

Assistant: That's pretty much it — except for the fact he took his life out of this world as a direct result of your punishment for prematurely bringing a life into this world.

God: That's... what's the word I'm looking for?

Assistant: Involuntarymanslaughter?

God: Shorter word.

Assistant: Ironic?

God: That's it. Ironic. Don't you think?

Assistant: Uh huh...

God: No?

Assistant: Yeah, yeah, it's ironic.

God: What's with that look?

Assistant: ...You've really changed. **B**

◆

Alan Zweibel's *latest book, a parody of the Haggadah titled* **For This We Left Egypt?**, *was co-written with Dave Barry and Adam Mansbach who are less Jewish than Alan.*

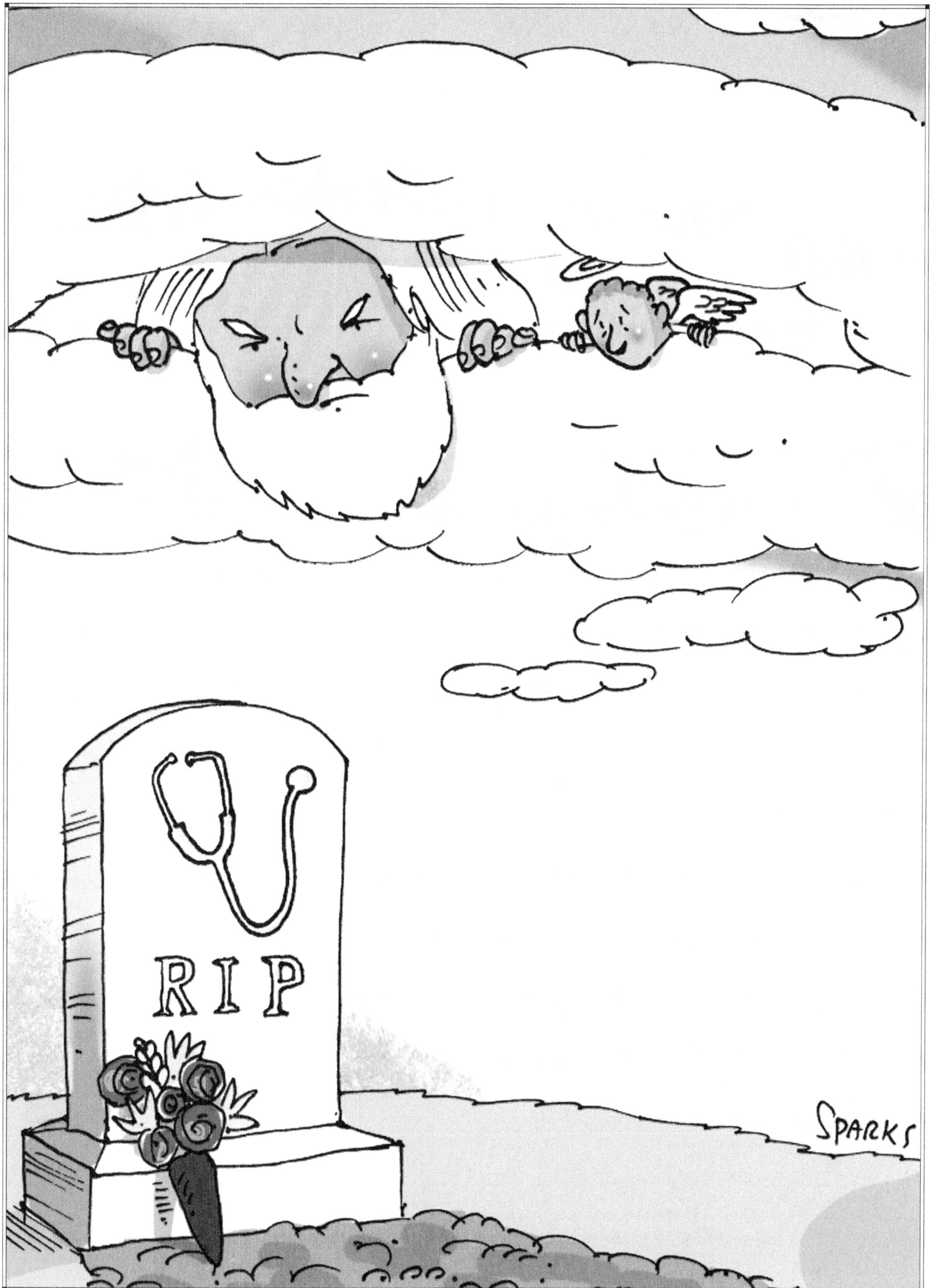
RIP
SPARKS

My Rat Story

Generally speaking, I enjoy the company of four-legged creatures more than I do my own species. When I look into the eyes of a dog or a cow or a three-toed sloth or even a jackal, I see only naïve good intentions. When I look into the eyes of my fellow human, I see silent displeasure with my haircut followed by as much false camaraderie as is needed to successfully convince me to give them a ride to the airport.

Where I currently live, on the Los Angeles coast, I am privileged to co-exist in proximity to quite a bit of California wild life: pelicans, coyotes, deer, seals, squirrels, possums, white women with cheekbone implants so identical they resemble a fossilized version of the children from *The Village of the Damned*.

There's also a large rat population. Like it or not, a few times a year some of them try to exercise squatter's rights in an effort to become my roommates. I've never fully adjusted to this idea.

But because I identify with Jane Goodall, I always make an earnest attempt to see them as tiny dogs, despite the fact that I'd never seen dogs of any size scoot straight up the wall or disappear under the dishwasher.

Why oh why, I often think, can't our species live together in peace? Then I remember: lice, fleas, Bubonic plague.

Yet in my research, I was delighted to learn that rats are friendly, altruistic and can become affectionate pets. I considered this option briefly. But I didn't feel ready to mentor a rat colony at that time. So I began to investigate the nonviolent methods available that would allow me to convince the rat population of my area to set up housekeeping elsewhere.

Thus did I invest in a "humane rat trap" — a simply constructed cage with a trap door that would allow me to capture any intruding rat unharmed. One at a time, I could then carry them to a pleasant, carefully chosen new place where they might continue their lives of friendly altruism uninterrupted.

RAT #1

It was 6 AM when I captured my first rat. I was awakened from a deep sleep by the faint clang of the door of the humane rat trap, on its perch near the breadbox on my kitchen counter.

Tiptoeing into the room, my first thought was: "Whoa! It worked! Why did we never try to do this with Santa?" That was before I noticed the look of terror on my captive's face. How had I become the kidnapper from *The Silence of the Lambs*? It hadn't occurred to me I'd have to cope with a confused and disturbed hostage.

Quickly I sprung into action, throwing an overcoat on top of my nightgown, picking up the cage by its convenient handle and heading out to the street to find an appropriate rat relocation site. This presented an interesting challenge since, sadly, no one on my block was looking for a rat to adopt.

As I walked away from my house, I gave some serious thought to releasing him into the yard of the contentious neighbor who lives directly behind me. On further reflection, I saw no reason to force a perfectly nice rat to start his brand new life under such unpleasant circumstances.

Instead I hiked six blocks up the hill to an idyllic-looking vacant lot full of construction materials, garbage and overgrown weeds. I then experienced a surprisingly emotional moment as I opened the gate to the humane rat trap and watched "my rat" run away safely, deep into what appeared to be a rat wonderland.

What a wonderful person I am, I thought as I headed home, humming the parts of "Born Free" that I could remember.

Later that morning, I was still patting myself on the back for my humanitarian efforts as I read the rest of an article on rat intelligence I had been meaning to finish. In it, I learned that our friends the rats all have something called "grid cells" — neurons in the cortex of their brain which emit

(continued)

⸻ ◆ ⸻

Merrill Markoe *has published eight books and written for a long list of television shows and publications, including the one you are holding.*

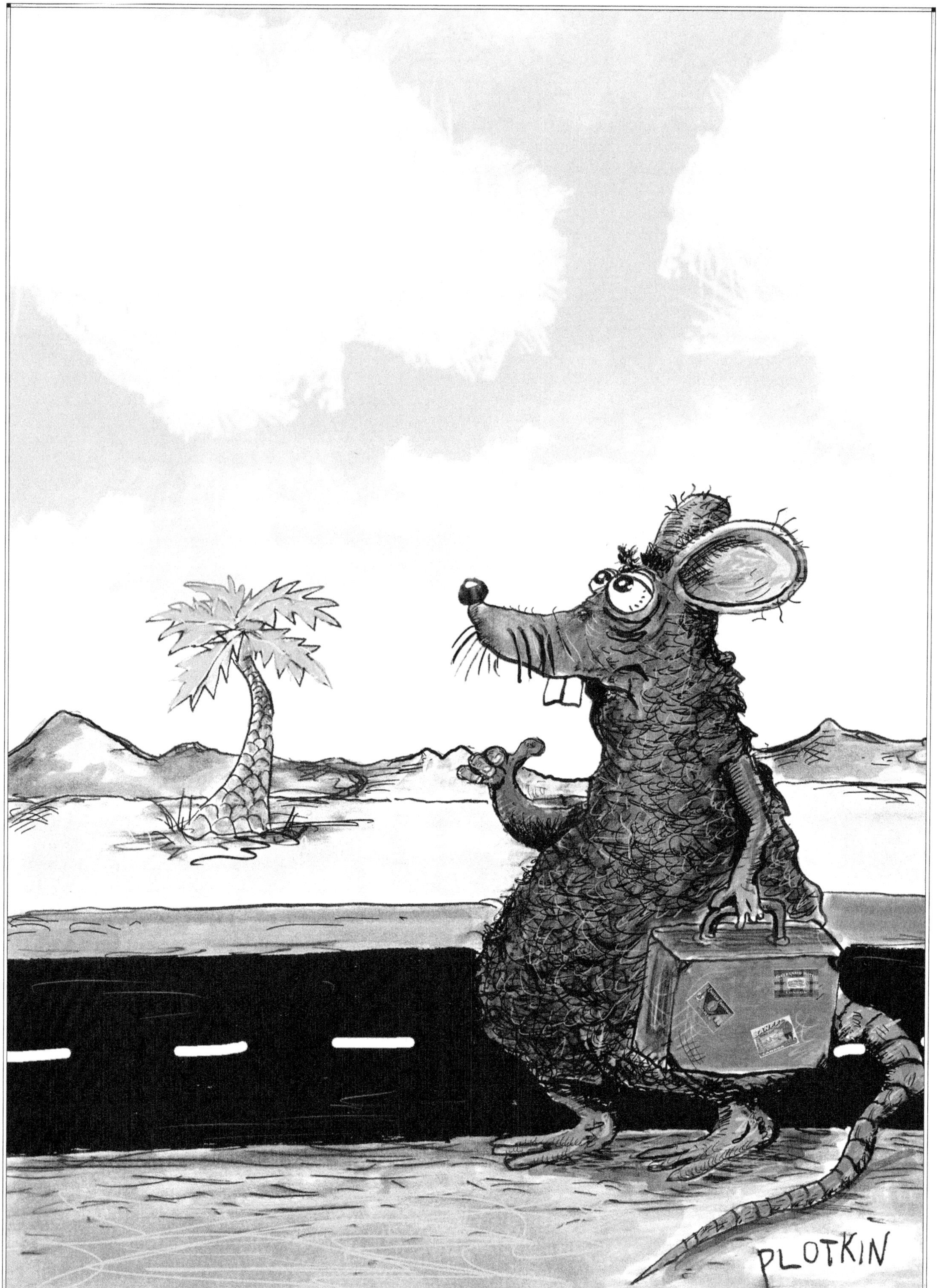
PLOTKIN

JONATHAN PLOKTIN

pulses of electricity allowing them to map and remember their movements over distances of up to ten miles.

If this was true, and I had no reason to believe it wasn't, I had basically airlifted my rat a couple of blocks down the street for a day of fresh air and sunlight. Apparently, thanks to his grid cells, he'd be returning to my place for supper.

As it turned out, that is exactly what happened.

Day Two

It was 4 AM when I caught him a second time. This time I let him "relax" for a few hours, until sunrise when I drove him ten miles away and dropped him off at the entrance to a state park.

"Remember to hydrate," I said, as I waved a fond goodbye.

That was it for rats and me until last week.

RAT #2

It was ten at night when I caught my second rat. This one presented me with an entirely different set of logistical problems.

First of all, from the moment of capture, all I could think about was that the ten-mile road trip he and I had ahead of us was not something I really wanted to do by myself at midnight. Concerned that I might not be able to keep an eye on the cage and drive at the same time, I decided to wait for my husband, Andy, to get home, then force him to accompany me.

As I sat alone in my kitchen, with my frightened prisoner staring at me, I was so overcome with empathy, I felt like a cold-hearted 19th-century industrial baron, throwing Jean Valjean off my land for having the nerve to pick through my slops to feed his poor family.

So moved was I by his plight, I put a small towel over his cage to help him stay calm in the face of such great disparity of wealth and power, just as I would have done for Jean Valjean himself.

When Andy arrived home around midnight, I greeted him at the door with the words every man longs to hear at the end of his day: "Let's go back out to the car. We have to drive ten miles to relocate a rat." Fortunately, he was a good sport as we placed the little towel-covered cage into the back of the CRV.

My plan was for us to drive straight down Pacific Coast Highway to the edge of the Malibu city limits, just far enough away to confuse the rat's grid cells.

As we peeled out of the driveway, our car made a sharp turn that caused the cage to totter a little. This ignited the time-honored *TECSIC* effect (tired, edgy couple squabbling in car).

"You should take the turns a little more carefully," I said, after a second strong turn and more rattling. "We have a prisoner back there, and I don't know how sturdy that cage is."

"When the clasp springs, the door

locks. Period. It's *locked*. Nothing can happen," Andy said in a tension-filled exhale as we hit the highway in silence.

As we drove, I monitored the odometer. At about mile six, I spotted an empty nursery beside a field. What a perfect setting for the viral video I was now planning to make where I'd release the rat, in slow motion, to the swelling theme from "Born Free."

And… something else.

There was a rat on my shoulder.

I made a noise like Curly from the Three Stooges.

"*Nyaaaaaaaa!* He's on me!" I shouted.

"No, he's not," said Andy, because he knew better (as men always do when couples argue in cars in the middle of the night).

"Yes, he is," I shrieked. "He's standing on my shoulder. Stop the car!"

"Merrill, get a grip," said Andy, determined to prove me wrong. "There's no rat on your shoulder… *Aaaaaaah!* Now he's on my shoulder! I'm pulling over!"

Opening the door, I jumped out of the car as we rolled to a stop.

"Get back in the car!" Andy said reflexively as I stood, stunned, in the right lane of the highway.

"No!" I said, "There's a rat loose in there."

"No, there's not," said Andy, for no reason at all as he opened his door so he could get out.

"There he goes!" I yelled as something scuttled across the hood.

I leapt back into the car, and we peeled back onto the road, worried now that, like the Robert De Niro character in *Cape Fear*, the rat was clinging to the underside of the car and having a thrill-ride back to the house with us.

Perhaps the relocation was successful. We haven't seen this rat again. And though I can't say I miss him, sometimes, late at night, I get a peaceful easy feeling as I imagine him telling his children, and maybe even his grandchildren (since rat gestation is only twenty-two days long) about how ruthless giant pink stormtroopers abducted him from his home.

I hope by now he understands I wasn't Pol Pot or Heinrich Himmler. I was The Green Lantern, only trying to help. **B**

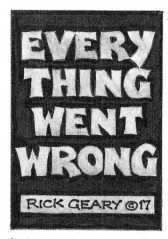

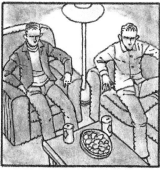

EVERY THING WENT WRONG
RICK GEARY ©17
I SPENT AN AFTERNOON RECENTLY AT THE HOME OF MY FRIEND NATE.
ALL WENT WELL UNTIL WE STARTED ARGUING POLITICS.
ON ANY OTHER SUBJECT HE IS USUALLY QUITE RATIONAL.
FINALLY, I FOUND IT NECESSARY TO BRAIN HIM WITH A TABLE LEG.
I'M SURE I LEFT FINGERPRINTS ALL OVER.
AS WELL AS TRACKS FROM MY DISTINCTIVE SNEAKERS.
BUS
IN MY AGITATED STATE, I BOARDED THE WRONG BUS...
WHICH DEPOSITED ME IN A FAR CORNER OF TOWN.
I PAUSED ON A BRIDGE TO DISPOSE OF MY SHOES AND THE TABLE LEG.
BUT AN ANGRY GUY STARTED YELLING AT ME ABOUT DUMPING TRASH IN THE RIVER.
I RAN FROM HIM AS FAST AS I COULD.
THEN THE CLOUDS BURST!
AS I RAN, I BEGAN COMPILING A MENTAL LIST...
OF ALL THE FOOLISH AND HEEDLESS THINGS I'VE DONE IN MY LIFE.
12
SUFFICE IT TO SAY I WAS LATE GETTING HOME.

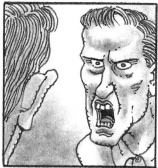

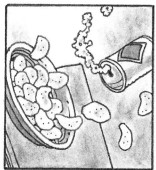

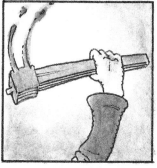

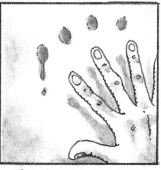

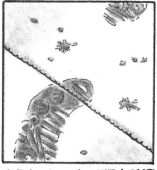

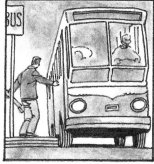

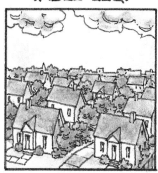

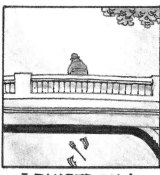

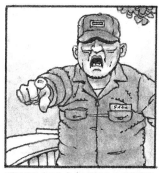

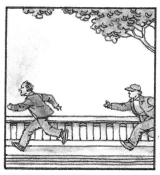

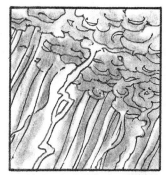

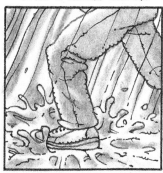

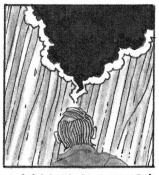

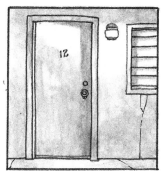

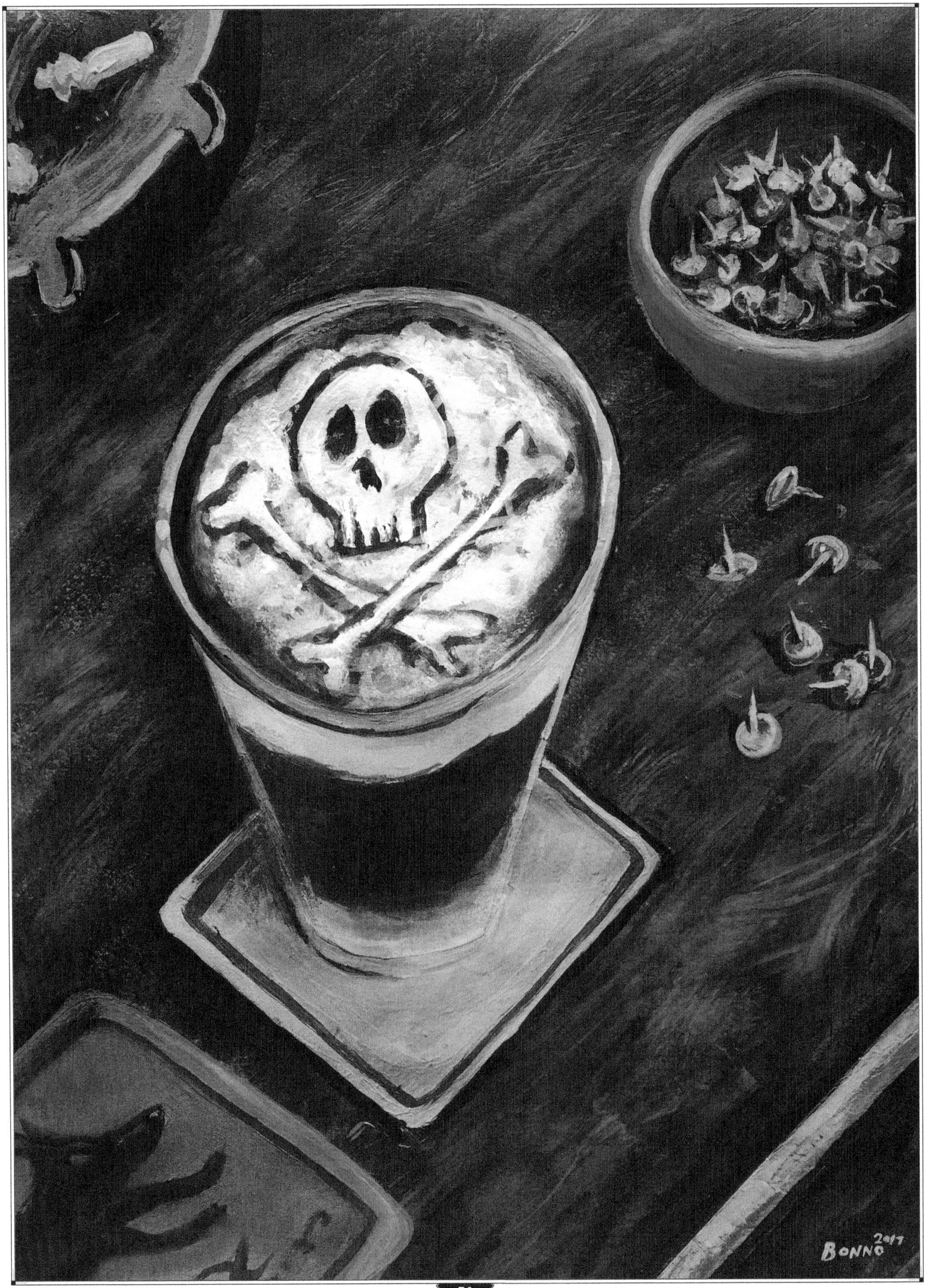
BONNO 2017

Eight NYC Bars You Need to Drink At Before You Die on Tuesday

New York City. You may like New Orleans, Austin or Chicago for your tipple, but no city in America offers more pound for pound and drink for drink than the Big Apple. In fact, the sheer volume and variety of choices can be overwhelming. But don't worry: We've taken the liberty of narrowing it down to eight watering holes that you absolutely must visit before you meet your untimely end this coming Tuesday. *Cheers!*

The Brandy Library

You'd be wise to reserve a table at this laid-back TriBeCa lounge, as only a limited number of patrons are allowed in to sample the Library's impressive selection of fine spirits and wines. If cocktails are more your thing, try The Dempsey—made with gin, calvados, anise and grenadine—or a gin fizz—which is basically the lifeblood of *Ronny Pulaski*, 42, a livery driver who will be picking you up at LaGuardia on Tuesday.

P.J. Clarke's

A Midtown stalwart known for its big burgers and expertly mixed Manhattans, Clarke's was depicted in the classic film *The Lost Weekend*, and has hosted many noteworthy people since it opened its doors in 1884. Among them: Frank Sinatra, Johnny Depp, Jackie Kennedy and *Maria "Kiki" Ortega*, 58, a sidewalk cellar door inspector who's fond of joking about how she's been phoning it in since being passed over for a promotion last year.

Gagopa

Frequently called "one of the greatest karaoke bars in America," Gagopa offers a seemingly endless songbook ranging from K-Pop to country…and neon-lit private rooms in which young revelers sing and drink and dance all night long, before emerging exhausted into the blinding light of morning and proceeding directly to their jobs at the city's largest scaffolding company.

Old Town Bar

Many a colorful character has bellied up to the long bar at this cavernous, time-honored establishment, including novelists, Broadway stars, politicians and local eccentrics, such as *Lester LaBarre*, 75, a wild-haired, self-taught painter who just dropped a banana peel on the edge of a crowded subway platform and kind of liked the way it made him feel.

The 21 Club

Originally a speakeasy, and still featuring a disappearing bar and a secret wine cellar from the old days, the 21 Club has long been a favored gathering spot for the city's elite and various wannabes. The latest is *Peter Singh*, 22, a heretofore unknown tech entrepreneur about to unleash a citywide "swarm" of experimental self-driving stretch limos to promote BRĒD, a new dating app exclusively for rich teenagers.

McSorley's

A charmingly dingy East Village haunt that serves only two kinds of beer — light and dark — McSorley's has served everyone from Abraham Lincoln, to Babe Ruth, to *Dani "Queen D" Beene*, 23, a paramedic who will be called into work unexpectedly on Tuesday night even though it's her birthday and she's been going at it pretty hard all day long, but that's okay because any asshole can drive an ambulance over a bridge in an ice storm.

Bemelmans Bar

Tucked away in the historic Carlyle Hotel, this cozy lounge features a mural by Ludwig Bemelmans, the creator of the classic Madeline children's books so beloved by Emily Alexander, 9, daughter of *Dr. Anna Rubenstein*, 41, a trauma surgeon taking Endofluxal, a heartburn drug whose side effects can include dizziness, nausea, violent spasms and a sudden compulsion to lock everyone else out of whatever room you're in.

Death + Company

Linda Yu, 26, drank here once. She liked it. That cool, dark, speakeasy vibe. The great craft cocktails, friendly people. It was everything she moved to New York City to experience—a world away from her old life back in Iowa. You come to a place like this, and you feel like you're in a movie. Even if in reality you're just a lowly part-time morgue worker about to be fired for misidentifying human remains. **B**

Memory's A Funny Thing

Daniel was not certain his father had remembered. Perhaps he had gotten the date wrong, or written down the name of the club incorrectly. Daniel had peered out discreetly into the crowd during the laughs and the applause breaks, but the stage lights made individuals indistinguishable. It would be typical of his father to make a big deal out of emailing for the information and then find a way to miss the show.

As he came off stage he met some strangers who had enjoyed his performance, then he saw Paul awaiting his attention, small and frail in his overcoat as though the weight of the wool itself might buckle the man's aging legs. Daniel disengaged from the knot of admirers and went to his father for a hug, a moment of genuine, human connection before the familial guards came up, the tensions, the mannerisms.

They stood awkwardly for a moment, assessing each other, shuffling. Paul said, "I need a cigarette. Can we . . .?" He trailed off with a gesture toward the door and together they stepped out of the warmth and into the alley.

"You're funny," Paul said.

"Thanks," Daniel said. Then, "I'm glad you could make it."

"You're much smarter than most of the guys who went on that stage tonight."

Daniel shrugged. He agreed, but it wasn't a thing he liked to say aloud. He preferred to mask his arrogance.

Paul sighed smoke. He blinked in a way that was almost a wince, almost a flinch. It told Daniel that he was trying not to say something or, more accurately, hoping to be coaxed.

Daniel did not know how not to oblige. He said, "What?"

Feigning confusion, Paul said, "What?" as though they were engaged in a Meisner exercise.

"There was something you wanted to say."

Paul nodded. He sighed again, shifted his head from side to side for a moment as though he was weighing options. Then he said, "I think you know."

Daniel thought he knew, too, but he'd been wrong before. He waited.

"There's a bit that you really have to stop doing."

Daniel had correctly surmised his father's thought. He knew which bit Paul was talking about. It was this:

The last time I visited my grandmother, Alzheimer's was just setting in. Every time she saw me she thought it was my birthday and gave me five dollars. It was exhausting to deal with. I had to keep walking in and out of that room.

(For the record, that is not a self-loathing anti-Semitic joke about a cultural relationship with money that values it above human decency. It's a self-loathing anti-capitalist joke about a societal relationship with money that values it above human decency.)

Grandma had just reached that point in the progression of the disease at which every conversation turns into a surreal 1970's television game show. She'd say, "I went into that place . . . with the buildings and the smell."

And we'd all shout, "Manhattan?"

"Yes! I was with that know-it-all lady with the flowered dress and the long boring stories."

"Your best friend, Katie?"

"Yes! We saw that horrible guy!"

"We need more clues!"

"He used to be horrible in New York, and then he was horrible all over the country and now he's horrible from space!"

"Howard Stern?"

"Yes!"

"Congratulations, grandma! You're going on to the Dementia Pyramid!"

"WHO ARE YOU PEOPLE?"

"Things you yell at the dinner table!"

(continued)

Dylan Brody *is a playwright and humorist, poet and snappy dresser.*
Don't ask him about his tie. He'll talk for an hour about the Plattsburgh knot.

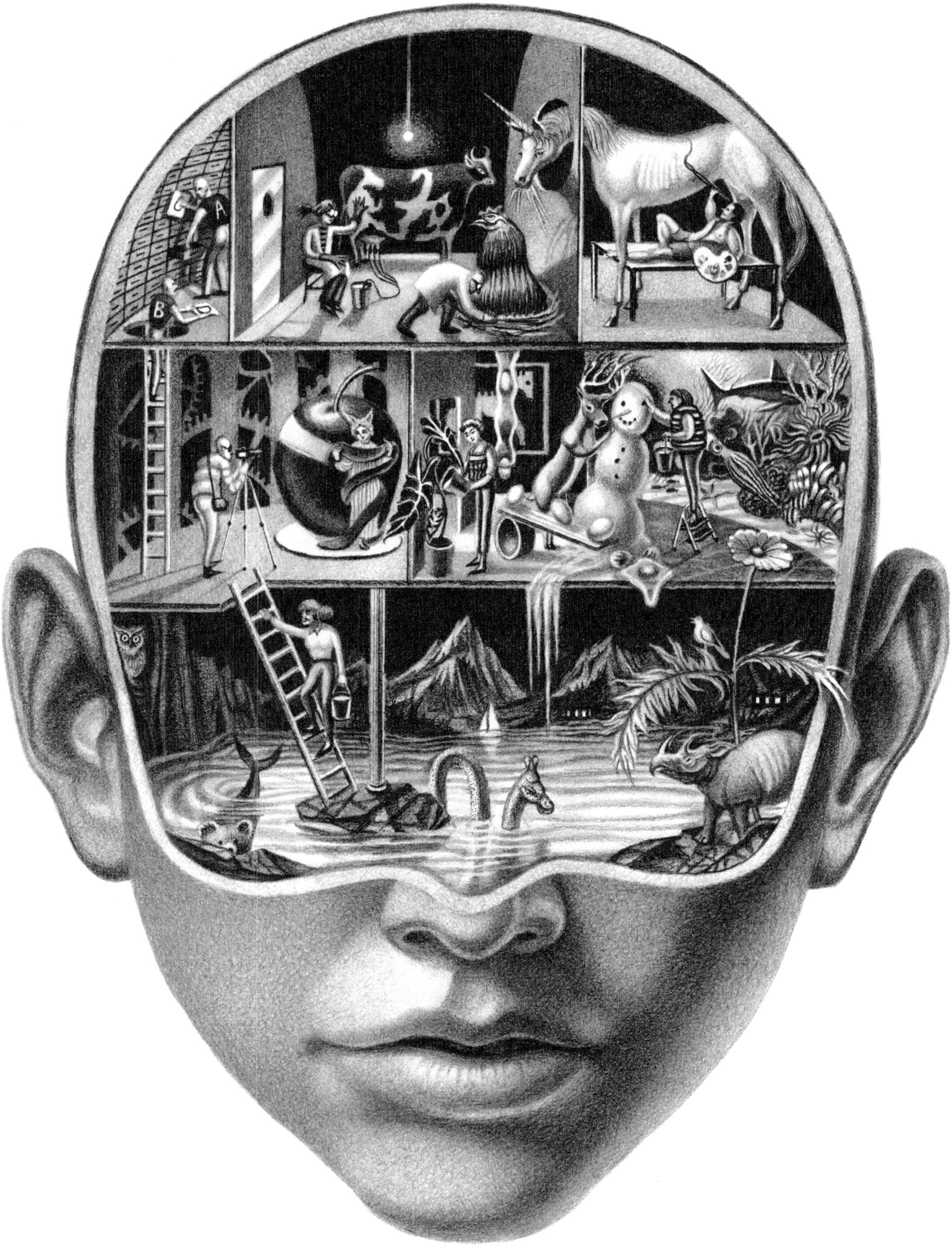
A
B

ARMANDO VEVE

"WHERE AM I?"

"Things you shout from the bathroom!"

"Ed Asner! Benjamin Netanyahu!"

"People you mistake for your dead husband? You've done it, Grandma! You've won Dementia Pyramid!"

After Grandma got bad, I remember my mother was all freaked out, realizing that she was facing a genetic crapshoot. She said, "Daniel, you have to tell me if I start showing symptoms so I'll know when it's time to take my own life."

I said, "Mom... we just had this conversation twenty minutes ago."

Daniel said to his father, hands in his pockets, shoulders up against the cold, "I wondered what you'd think of that."

Paul said, "It's not funny."

"It gets a lot of laughs. And a huge applause break."

"That doesn't mean it's funny. It would destroy your mother if she saw it."

"She can handle more than you think."

"It's about her mother."

"Yes."

Paul pulled smoke. His pressed his lips together. "It's really offensive."

"Different people are offended by different things."

"I think you've forgotten how awful it was."

Daniel said, "No."

"It wasn't cute, Danny. It wasn't funny. It was tragic."

That was when, with absolute certainty, Daniel knew he was right and his father was wrong.

In 1974, Daniel was ten years old. He went with his parents and his sister to visit Grandma and Grandpa at their home in New Jersey for a big, tense Thanksgiving dinner. This was long before his grandmother's mind began to slip. Long pauses raised family dynamics to a silent vibration. Daniel's mother bathed in a lifetime of familial subtext. Daniel's father tried to imagine the many ways he was being judged by his in-laws. In order to avoid putting another bite of inedible, turkey-flavored particle board into his mouth, Daniel said: "This summer I'm going to camp! I'm gonna ride horses and learn to play guitar!"

His grandmother shot back, "I went to a camp once." Before the Alzheimer's, she was a *tummler*. A good one.

Grandpa laughed sharply; Daniel's parents, Paul and Ellen, gasped. His sister, Franny, stared at her food. When things made people laugh, she went quiet as though she had to analyze every word

"We at the Internal Revenue Service are cognizant that the individual citizen, in many cases, pays more tax than some of the larger corporations... nonetheless we also feel that we have a good thing going."

in careful silence.

Grandma went on with barely a pause. "Spent nine months of my life in a yard full of Gypsies and queers playing liar's poker." With a deliberate gesture, she rolled up a sleeve to look at the numbers tattooed on her forearm. She said, "Pair of threes." She paused, looking at an imagined opponent — then frowned. "Three fives."

Grandpa laughed now in a way that was joyous and actively supportive as he saw the discomfort on the faces of Daniel's parents.

Paul said: "Stop it, Sally. That's terrible."

Ellen sighed; Paul's jaw tensed with a seething rage. Daniel watched it all, sorting out as best he could the source of his parents' discomfort, trying to reverse-engineer the backstory that made his grandmother's joke so potent.

Grandpa, always ready to put horror under laughing glass, grinned at his wife. He said to Daniel's parents, or perhaps to Daniel himself: "That's when I fell in love with her — do you know how sharp you have to be to win with the same numbers every day? Besides, I always liked skinny girls."

Paul clenched out a low, "Come on, man," and it sounded like some sort of warning. He glanced toward Daniel and Franny, hoping his father-in-law would censor himself. But Grandpa would not be silenced; he would not be quieted by the squeamish man who had married his daughter. "I saw her across the yard and I thought: *My God. Her tights are loose!*" He took a beat to let the shock register on the faces of Paul and Ellen. "...then I realized she wasn't wearing tights."

That image made Daniel laugh a little; Grandma fell apart with giggles.

Ellen said: "Really, guys. This is wrong. Set an example. You don't make jokes about tragedy."

Grandma feigned anger, but Daniel could see her inner glee. She said: "Oh, Ellen, no! We're Jews. We don't believe in tragedy. We believe in horror, atrocity and injustice — and we recognize them all as inherently hilarious."

At that Grandpa laughed, and even Paul, so Ellen raised her hands in surrender. If it was to be a battle of jokes, she knew she could not compete.

Then Grandma with an urgency that startled Daniel, a seriousness that seemed

D. WATSON

survival, it was their ability to remember, and still to feel joy. The miracle was that their laughter was genuine and warm, not manic.

So on the sidewalk outside the club, he said to his father: "Grandma said we're Jews. We don't believe in tragedy."

Paul snorted and smoke came with it. "She also said, 'Never forget.' Look where that got her."

Daniel chuckled. "That's funny!"

"Don't use it," Paul said.

"Only if you promise that you will," Daniel said.

"What? You mean in conversations?"

"Maybe you can sneak it into an academic treatise on the danger of cliché. Or when you're talking to your therapist about how insensitive and inappropriate your son is."

Paul shook his head. He stamped his feet in the cold as though it could warm him up. He pulled on the cigarette as though that could warm him up.

Daniel said, "Do you remember the Thanksgiving she told me that? That we don't beelive in tragedy? She and Grandpa were doing shtick together. You and Mom were very upset."

"I think I've blocked most of those Thanksgivings. They were... difficult."

""That's why I have to filter it all through jokes, Dad. All the horror. All the loss. All the injustice. It's the only way to preserve it. Without the lens, it hurts too much. Without the jokes, you have to forget. That's what they were telling me. That's why they were so, so funny together. You don't remember that conversation?"

Paul shrugged. Those holidays had been problematic, Ellen's parents always judging him for his lack of financial savvy, poking at him for the years he had spent barely supporting her and the kids before he got his footing. The overcooked, overly ostentatious meals that served as a passive-aggressive demonstration of decadent opulence. The dirty jokes that were supposed to seem risqué and naughty rather than vulgar just because they came from people with gray hair instead of construction workers.

"You muttered and cursed about them all the way home in the station wagon." Daniel said, chuckling, "It was pretty hilarious."

Paul shrugged, unable to find the humor. He said, "I don't remember." **B**

incongruous with the exchange, leaned across the table and poked at the side of his head with a stiff finger. "Never forget."

Daniel hadn't. He had remembered every moment of the conversation and, over the years, he had understood

with increasing wonder just what his grandparents were so funny about. As he learned their history, and the larger history of which they had been a part, the series of jokes came into focus one at a time until he realized that the miracle of his grandparents was not their mere

The *Charlie Hebdo* of American Satire

The Realist (1958-2001) was the legendary satirical magazine published by Paul Krassner — provocateur, radical, yippie, prankster — that struck from below with humor and ridicule. Outrageous cartoons were the highlight of each issue — some of the most incendiary ever to appear in an American magazine.

The Realist Cartoons collects for the very first time the best drawings from the magazine's historic run, including work by R. Crumb, Art Spiegelman, S. Clay Wilson, Jay Lynch, Wallace Wood, Trina Robbins, Mort Gerberg, Jay Kinney, Wallace Wood, Trina Robbins, Richard Guindon, Nicole Hollander, Skip Williamson, and many others.

"Paul Krassner is an activist, a philosopher, a lunatic and a saint, but most of all he is funny."
— Lewis Black

"Skin So Thin, It's Inside Out"

Ethan Persoff talks with *Paul Krassner* about running *The Realist*, hacking *The New York Times* best-seller list, and that "true, extraordinary liar," Donald Trump.

.... ◆ ....

*I*n the late Fifties, three things radically changed the course of American comedy: Lenny Bruce, The Second City and The Realist. From its first issue in the spring of 1958, Paul Krassner's iconoclastic "journal of freethought and satire" created a comedic template that is still being followed today; its mix of fact and intelligent opinion delivered with a mordant, knowing skepticism is as current as John Oliver and as omnipresent as the entire internet. But you don't hear much about The Realist these days — it's the fate of truly seminal sources to seem inevitable, when in fact they reshaped the world in their own image.

Fortunately, in 2006 Krassner teamed with archivist/comic artist Ethan Persoff on The Realist Archive Project (www.ep.tc/realist/), a free online repository of every issue of the magazine from its 43-year run. They recently collaborated again on a deluxe coffee table book, The Realist Cartoons, published by Fantagraphics.

The election of Donald Trump seemed to be a particularly Krassnerian moment, so I asked Ethan to call Paul and ask a few leading questions. — MG

ETHAN PERSOFF: Paul, what's your opinion of Trump?

PAUL KRASSNER: Where to begin? Personally, for me, it goes back to when George Bush won the presidency in 2000. That was due to the Electoral College, even though Al Gore had won the popular vote.

That same time, Hillary Clinton was elected senator. She announced, publicly, the first thing she was going to do was get rid of the Electoral College.

Years later, I was doing a column for *The New York Press*, and I sent Clinton a letter asking her about the status of her promise. She didn't reply.

During the campaign, Trump called Clinton a crook —

EP: Right, "Lock her up".

PK: — he called her a crooked businessperson. But that's what *he* was. Everything he says about anybody is really about him.

He's a true, extraordinary liar.

EP: What's your opinion of his "fake news" media scolding?

PK: Another example of projection. He calls the newspapers dishonest, because he is, in fact, the most dishonest.

Trump became an insanely narcissistic dictator once he won, bragging about his electoral numbers as proof. But prior to that, he endlessly insisted the Electoral College was a sham. That, to me, wins the prize for irony.

EP: I have to wonder, what if Clinton had won the electoral count, but lost the popular vote?

PK: Oh, then he would have said it was rigged.

EP: Lock her up!

PK: When I wrote the letter to her, it was partly because I'd heard the Electoral College was based on slavery.

EP: And there's gerrymandering, which is also racist.

PK: Yes. You know, the thing with Trump, is there's talk of anything from impeachment, assassination, treason ... But that leads to more irony, because that would leave President Pence. Pence has just as much an interest in turning evolution around, and going back to barbaric times, but has the ability to pass as sane. Trump can't do that.

EP: Do you think Trump's madness is an asset to his opposition? He's such an easily identifiable lunatic, does that provide for a sense of protection, as opposed to Pence, who is so much more canny and quiet?

PK: There's fear of Trump, and then there's dictatorship in action. The things he's been doing are disgusting -- these appointments! Like Rick Perry for Department of Energy. It's so insane. And then, Betsy DeVos. No education experience ... I think even starting in kindergarten. *(Laughter)*

EP: Yes. Everyone has their own personal thing that they're scared about with Trump. Me, it's the environment. I can't believe his appointment of Scott Pruitt with the EPA.

PK: They're all horrible. Then there's Michael Flynn. He is the core of the hypocrisy of the relationship between Trumpo the Elephant and Putin. *(continued)* 🕿

EP: What's your take on Trump and Russia?

PK: I read one article where an unidentified Russian official used the phrase "useful idiot." That's really what it is.

It's like J. Edgar Hoover; he stayed around for decades [via] blackmail. I think it's the same thing. You don't have to say it, you know. Hoover would just go to JFK and say "We found some photo of you in bed with Marilyn Monroe. But don't you worry, we'll keep it in our safe."

EP: You've lived through some Red scares; can you imagine any other time where this Russia stuff would be forgiven?

PK: I think foreign countries may have influenced previous elections. I don't know, but it was mostly *before* the technology of the internet. So, if there's no internet, there ain't no hackin'. It's like there ain't no divorce if you don't have no marriage! Whatever deal was made, or hacked, I think Trump decided to run the night of the 2011 Washington Correspondents' Dinner. Obama had *such good jokes* that night. But the camera was on Trump, and you could see that he was *foaming*.

EP: That shot of him is amazing. The video of Trump's boiling back head. It's really gorgeous.

PK: Humiliation makes a difference. You know, years before any of this, Trump developed his *modus operandi* for media/political success: You cheat. What pushed him into public profile was the stated success of his book, *The Art of the Deal*. But what I found out is that he bought 20,000 copies of his own book from Random House, and that made it a *New York Times* best-seller.

Similarly, L Ron Hubbard had his book *Dianetics*. He had a Scientologist working at *The New York Times* who had access to the details of their best-sellers lists. Back then, there was a list of cities that the *Times* measured sales at particular bookstores. So, Hubbard didn't have to buy 20,000 copies, he just had his spy tell him where to buy several copies at those locations, and the Church of Scientology had an instant "best-seller".

EP: Earlier you mentioned two interesting words: "assassination" and "impeachment." You have the benefit of having lived through Kennedy and Nixon.

PK: My earliest remembrance of a president was Franklin D Roosevelt.

EP: Do you remember him on the radio?

PK: Yes. He was famous for having his Fireside Chats. Which, through these decades, has evolved into tweets.

EP: Here's a very pointed question: When Kennedy got shot — what's your memory of that?

PK: Several memories. One was my first wife was out shopping, heard it on somebody's radio, and immediately bought a TV set. That's one thing I remember, just being glued to the television…And I was getting calls, maybe not that day, but from

Cartoon by Wende, from The Realist #37, *Sept. 1962.*

people wanting to write an article about the conspiracy aspect of it. You know of Jean Shepherd, right?

EP: Of course.

PK: He was a big influence on me. He said, "This will change the whole country." He thought it was a coup. And it turned out that the CIA had the Mafia do it. After all of my studying about it, that's what it was. The Mafia were the puppets of the puppeteer in that.

I would listen to Jean Shepherd every night, and he said — he *predicted* – that America would have a dictator who won the presidency because he came out of show business. And it happened. You know, [Trump's] not like Ronald Reagan, who came out of Hollywood, of course. But in Reagan's case, he couldn't make the distinction between reality and his

movie roles. But he did say he was willing to take a senility test! Of course, the suggestion that he'd take a senility test is a suggestion that you already are senile.

EP: Right. That's very funny.

PK: Jumping back to Trump. Along the same lines of the buying the 20,000 copies of his book, the first day of his presidential campaign, he came down the Trump Tower elevator. There were people with placards, saying "TRUMP 2016" — but they were all hired actors. Fifty of 'em.

EP: You know, the success of that red hat really disturbs me. It's so idiotic — but it really seemed to work.

PK: I agree. No other presidential candidate had a cap like that. And a slogan. I've seen people on TV asked, "What do you think about the election?" One elderly woman said: "Oh it's wonderful! We're going to Make America Great Again!"

EP: How could they win on a campaign of awful messages? Maybe Steve Bannon is some AD&D wizard, casting a spell that everything negative becomes positive. "Trust me, Trump: Kick babies instead of kiss them. It'll work!"

PK: I agree that's possible. But it's narcissism that made Trump do this. Narcissism with skin so thin, it's inside out.

That's what he was doing, too, during the campaign. If your skin is inside out, then it's projecting. Hillary "was a crook," but *he* was. He called Bernie Sanders "crazy" and *he* was. "Lyin' Ted Cruz"…

EP: Why do you think those nicknames were so effective? It seemed, once you were labeled by him, you were done.

PK: Bush had his nicknames, but they were favorable. He called Karl Rove his —

EP: "Turd Blossom"!

PK: Right, "Turd Blossom" …and he *was*.

EP: The prettiest turd.

PK: Regarding Trump's narcissism, here's my favorite joke: Trump was in the elevator of Trump Tower. It stopped on one floor and a woman got in. She said: "Oh! You're Donald Trump! Oh my, I would love to give you a blow job. I really would. I have a great reputation. I will make it that you will never forget this blow job. I really am good. I practice a lot. And I want to give you a blow job so much."

And Trump says, "Yeah, but what's in it for *me*?"

(laughter)

There's an old saying in psychology. In order to deceive people, you have to deceive yourself. Here's the thing: Trump has *instant* belief. He just *believes* whatever he says. With Obama's birth certificate controversy, he would *believe it*, even though he had to *know* it wasn't true. Then, he said he'd *hired investigators* to go to Hawaii.

EP: *(embarrassed for history)* I remember that.

PK: I think that was a lie, too! I don't think he ever sent them. Or, if he *did* send them, and they didn't find any "evidence," then he lied by omission...of facts.

EP: I wonder if these lies are going to have consequences — if impeachment will happen. Getting Congress to do it will be nearly impossible.

PK: There's little hints that the Republicans — their conscience is getting 'em. Those are my hopes.

EP: The fear I have is we're going to lose this country through this motherfucker. That we're going to have a police state — that we won't have a free press. Do you think these are real fears?

PK: Oh, yeah. Well, you know, a police state has a bad reputation. I mean, cops love it!

The thing is — ever since I took a lot of acid — I have become an overdoer of being optimistic. You can pick your metaphor, but I think Trump's a blessing in disguise.

With these scares, he's the monster — the Frankenstein — that we've created. It's from the country's dumbing-down of the media. Especially with the commercials. You know, when they first had TV news, they didn't have commercials.

EP: I've been trying to get more into the habit of watching *PBS News Hour*. It's amazing to have a full hour of commercial-free news, and not looping news, like CNN. What's sad is I find I have to build up the stamina for it. I actually find myself wanting commercial breaks. PBS had less coverage of Trump's campaign, too. Probably because there were no ads to sell.

PK: The epitome of it, regarding coverage of Trump, was CEO Leslie Moonves, who said, "It may not be good for America, but it's damn good for CBS!"

EP: You know, the week Trump won, to deal with shock, my mind started remembering things that made me laugh. One of your stories showed up: The one when you met Bob Dylan and asked for his opinion about the Holocaust.

PK: I was at a radio show. And he was watching in the room. It was me, Abbie Hoffman, a rabbi and some others. During the panel, the Holocaust was integrated into the dialogue. Dylan was there watching, sitting in a dark corner in the back of

Cartoon by Mort Gerberg, from The Realist #50*, May 1964.*

the room. When the program was over, he walked up and said to me, "You didn't say much." And I thought that was funny, because *he* was such a minimalist.

Then I held up my fist, like a microphone, and asked, "So, what do you think about the Holocaust?" He offered his minimalistic reply: "I resented it."

EP: That's just too good a joke.

PK: I remember that, more than the radio panel, because it had such an essence of itself.

EP: That's the benefit of minimalism, right? It's like these insane Trump tweets. In some way, they're stronger because they're just 140 characters.

PK: By the way, did you see Anderson Cooper laugh for five minutes when Kellyanne Conway used the phrase "alternative facts"? It was such a bizarre

oxymoron, he couldn't stop laughing.

EP: My favorite one of her's is the Bowling Green Massacre. The internet was hilarious on that. For the Holocaust, of course, it's "Never Forget"; so, for the Bowling Green Massacre, people were posting pictures of green bowling balls, with the phrase "Never Remember."

PK: Oh, that's good. It's like what I was mentioning about optimism. The answer is what we saw right after the inauguration, with the march and the rallies. Trump is essentially the monster we've created. Whereas Frankenstein was made from corpses, Trump was made from fringe subcultures: First from the white supremacists ... Trump was on the radio with some insane conspiracy theorist, and the host said, "My listeners, they really *love you*."

Trump then went to the evangelists, 'cause that was another subculture. He couldn't think of anything, the first time, from the Bible. Next time, though, he brought a Bible with him. He was smart enough to take the cellophane off it.

EP: I think for the most part, you've always been on the right side of history, actions you've taken and political/moral positions — everything from civil rights to women's rights to drug freedom. But I don't know how you decided to do some of this shit. For example, you ran an abortion referral service inside *The Realist*. No reward beyond a moral victory.

PK: Back then, when it was illegal, people thought doctors who performed abortions should be arrested and convicted.

EP: Let's discuss the development of your ethics. What's your internal compass? Have you always had these instincts?

PK: It happens organically. I remember when *Look* magazine said about abortion, "There are no humane doctors ... all of them are just in it for the money." And I knew of one: Dr. Spencer in Ashland, Pennsylvania. He had a reputation. It turned out, to be, also, that he was a subscriber.

So, I wrote him a letter, asking for an interview, because I wanted to point out that *Look*'s statement was a lie. And I promised him that I would go to prison

The Disneyland Memorial Orgy, *by Paul Krassner and Wallace Wood, published in the May 1967 issue of* The Realist. *Readers with annoying bare patches on their wall can buy a copy at* www.paulkrassner.com *for $35 plus shipping and handling.*

sooner than identify him.

EP: Was that a concern of his?

PK: I just volunteered it. So that he would know. And he allowed me to interview him, albeit anonymously.[1]

When I published the interview, I started to get calls. Women who were pregnant that didn't want to be, and didn't know where to go. These were different ages, different classes. I remember one that really had the most force to it: A nurse called. And she couldn't get a doctor to help her. From a hospital, or even privately.

So, I referred her to Dr. Spencer. And she sent me a gift. She knew I had a little daughter. And she sent me a doll. A lion. Holly, my daughter, named it Lenny the Lion, after Lenny Bruce.

EP: Oh, that's great.

PK: I began to get more and more calls, and I couldn't say no. You know this is not an abstract placard saying "Peace Now", this was somebody that I could help. I couldn't say no — 'cause there are so many things going on in the world that you *can't* help.

I never *thought* I'd become an under-

ground abortion referral service. But, you know, it became my calling, in a way.

EP: How long did you continue to help people out?

PK: I stopped when I moved to San Francisco [in 1971]. By that time there were others doing referrals — Protestant ministers. So, I left my practice behind me.

EP: *The Realist* was one of the first, if not the first, news sources to talk about Enovid [the first birth control pill].

PK: In the first few issues! And the pill was just a rumor. This guy, a journalist — I didn't pay him much — he did a two-part article, I think I paid him $100 for each. He went to Puerto Rico, where they were testing women. I had mixed feelings about this, because they were testing them like guinea pigs. But it worked, and it became known as "the Pill."

EP: Since we're referring to a lot of issues of *The Realist*, we should probably mention the online archive. I recall, with some humor and business sense, you only asked one thing: That we edit the image to the Disneyland Orgy to include a link to your site, saying a poster was available for sale on your website.

PK: Oh yeah, that was a *pure* ad.

EP: The first ad to run in *The Realist*,

probably?

PK: Well, sure. *(laughs)* It was letting people know the poster existed.

EP: In the 10 years that the archive's been up, it's enjoyed a lot of regular traffic and is now referenced in many dissertations. By the way, did you see the *Washington Post* article linking to the archive, specifically the LBJ story?[2]

PK: Oh, yeah. I heard about that from Harry Shearer. He sent me the link to the article, where they refer to me as an "obscure 1960s figure." The subject line of Harry's email was "It's official!" and then in the message, a link to the article and the words "you're obscure!" I laughed hysterically.

I think the LBJ piece ("The Parts Left Out of the Kennedy Book," *The Realist* #74, May 1967) is still the most notorious article; people remember it. Lewis Black said he was 14 when he read it and said he was shocked! You know, because the article was written as a seduction, in a way. To the culmination, to the... what do they call it in sex? The climax!

And then I published the anagram for Nixon's veep's name, Spiro Agnew.

---

[1] "An Impolite Interview With An Abortionist," *The Realist* #35, June 1962.

[2] "Trump's presidency is doomed," *The Washington Post*, Jan. 16, 2017.

EP: "Grow a penis." Do you remember how that got published?

PK: It was originally a guy from *Life*. He'd interviewed me, and mentioned some of the staffers had seen *Rosemary's Baby*, where there's an anagram moment with Scrabble pieces, something to do with witchcraft —

EP: "Steven Marcato".

PK: Yeah. Staffers had discovered this joke about the vice president's name, based on that scene. They couldn't use it in *Life*, but it had to go somewhere. So, I ran it in the four-page comic that Richard Guindon and I did together.[3]

EP: Both the LBJ piece and Rosemerica comic clearly bend into surrealism. The response of readers, delighted and *infuriated*, had to be one of the best moments of your life.

PK: Many, many people believed [the LBJ piece], even for just a moment. It was something I'd learned from Joseph Heller, when I interviewed him (*Realist* #39). I asked about one of the patients in *Catch-22*, who is in a veterans hospital. The patient was wrapped up like a mummy, fed through IV's, excreting through tubes — he was just a middleman for digestion. I asked Heller, and he said, "Well you know, it's possible, but not probable."

EP: "Possible, but not probable" explains these last 15 months on Earth.

PK: Regarding the LBJ piece, there were people who claimed to remember a photograph! *(laughs)*

People who said they believed the article, if only for a moment, included

[1]"Rosemerica's Baby," *The Realist* #93, August 1972.

Daniel Ellsberg, who released The Pentagon Papers. He said the reason he believed it, was because he just so much *wanted* it to be true.

EP: Speaking of Ellsberg, and now Trump, how do you feel about leaking?

PK: Well, I leak several times a day. *(Shared laughter)*

EP: It's very good for you.

PK: That's bladder control.

EP: It's funny that the Russian sex blackmail was Trump having a urine party with a bunch of hookers.

PK: That was a fake. But it became a perfect image for comedians worldwide.

EP: But it's like the LBJ issue — maybe it will stick. People also remember The Disneyland Orgy from the magazine. And the wonderful FUCK COMMUNISM poster.

PK: You know, I use a walker, but I go to the gym three times a week, to use the treadmill. I had my FUCK COMMUNISM T-shirt on, you know, the red, white and blue. As I was walking out, there was a policeman who held the door open for me. And he saw the T-shirt.

EP: Oh, God —

PK: He said, "Hey, that's a great T-shirt!" He took it literally!

EP: I know the poster was said to be the perfect confluence of two banned terms.

PK: Kurt Vonnegut praised it for that.

EP: "Fuck" has kind of won, right? You can say "fuck" anything now, and it's fine. That is one experience I don't have, growing up when that word was so verboten. I understand how saying "Fire" in a crowded theater is illegal, but I don't have an understanding of a world where saying "Fuck" could get you arrested.

How did Lenny Bruce work around it?

PK: He had to use a euphemism. He'd have to say "frig."

The first time I met Lenny, he came to New York, and he called — because *The Realist* was his favorite magazine.

EP: That had to feel great.

PK: It did. Steve Allen was the first subscriber. He would give subscription gifts to several friends, and Lenny was one of them.

Lenny then sent a lot of subscriptions to his friends. That's how it started, and how it grew — word of mouth — which is better than advertising, because it's free and you're getting it from someone you know, an individual.

When I met Lenny for the first time, I gave him an advance copy of an interview with Dr. Albert Ellis, a psychologist. Lenny was reading and said "He used the word ['fuck']!" I explained to him that Ellis had a campaign that "fucking was good" therefore, if you wanted to say something unfriendly, you should say "unfuck you"...

Lenny asked, "How does he get away with this?" I told him, "The Supreme Court said use of the word wasn't obscene in a magazine if it was a redeeming social value, and no prurient interest."

Lenny asked: "What's that? Prurient?" He went to his suitcase on his bed in the hotel room. Inside was a huge unabridged dictionary. At first, it said something like "itching" — and Lenny asked, "Is this something like a novelty store?"

EP: Where they sell the powder!

PK: Or the dribble glasses. But the second definition was "arousal of sexuality."

Created in 1963 by Paul Krassner and John Francis Putnam, this poster was a staple of dorm rooms for decades. Kurt Vonnegut called it "a miracle of compressed intelligence nearly as admirable for potent simplicity, in my opinion, as Einstein's e=mc²."

ADDITIONAL COPIES AVAILABLE FROM THE MOTHERS OF THE AMERICAN REVOLUTION, WASHINGTON, D.C.

Lenny was performing that night at Town Hall. He asked me to hand out copies of *The Realist*, with the Ellis interview, in front of the theater. From then on, Lenny thought that his act would be protected, because it had redeemable social value. But that's not the way prosecutors felt about it.

EP: Right. The conspiracy theory I've heard is that it's because he took on the Catholic Church.

PK: Oh, absolutely. Absolutely right. His "Religions, Inc" piece got him in a lot of trouble. The reason he got busted for obscenity was there wasn't a law against *blasphemy*, but that's what he was really arrested for.

EP: You know when Scott Marshall and I were putting together the Lenny Bruce tribute in the Wilcock comic, we included John Wilcock's experience with Lenny. You're in a few panels. It's been fun to find opportunities to include you in the comic — you're in five scenes now.

I have sort of a funny agreement with John: If he can't recall the full story, or dialogue, I can fill in the details.

PK: Oh (laughs), well. that's trusting.

EP: You both are very trusting people! He couldn't remember verbatim exchanges with you from 1961. So, we gave the joke from you to be "Lenny would be a big fan of your *couch*, John."

PK: That's funny. When I saw that in your comic, I remembered saying it! I remembered something that didn't happen. Now I have something in common with Kellyanne Conway.

It's something I would have done. You made up something real.

EP: Thank you. I only do that in a few panels to keep everything glued together as a story. Otherwise it's just a bunch of disconnected fragments.

PK: Too close to reality, then.

EP: How do you think Lenny would respond to Trump?

PK: I think he would do it as a really high form of satire. He would make Trump a hero — in the sense that he would take a different approach. I'm saying that because he did that about Adolf Eichmann, the Nazi organizer. Lenny would say, "He was doing his job!" He would just take an approach like that. Lenny would "appreciate" the defined tragedy.

I think Bill Maher's show, Feb. 17,

[1]See *The American Bystander* #1, Dec. 2015.

was terrific. Lenny would have really appreciated it. Just the same way Lenny got serious sometimes, and the audience would say, "Hey, you're honest!" instead of "Hey, you're funny." Maher's monologue that night was really beautiful. Because he's well informed, and he couldn't just do jokes about it. He talked about the fascism. He talked about the dangers. It was just brilliant presentation of the seriousness of fascism in action.

EP: What do you think Abbie Hoffman would do about Trump?

PK: Oh, I think he would do the same thing as Maher. Abbie really had a sense of humor that was spontaneous. And it was based on being well informed. Bill Maher was doing that. He was rabble-rousing. He was trying to let people know how serious it was.

EP: I can't help but feel such sadness that Abbie is gone. You mentioned Shepherd as an influence, for me it's Abbie, who I regret never knowing personally. You read his books and every page glows. He's such a wonderful soul and gifted writer. Do you recall going to rallies with Abbie?

PK: I remember we had taken some acid in his home, and got a call that some Puerto Rican kids had gotten busted for pot. Abbie said, "Okay, we gotta go there." Show them the hippies respected the kids who were busted. Because they were Puerto Rican kids. So, as we're walking there Anita, Abbie's wife at the time, mentioned she was going to regurgitate from the acid. And I said to her, "You can just vomit over by the curb over there, and we'll stand around you." That we'd hide her. Abbie said, "Now *that's* community!"

There were lots of things like that. We saw a police car, full of four cops, two in the front and two in the back, and Abbie yelled, "You guys on a double date?"

I told him he reminded me of Lenny, and he said: "Oh *really*? He's my God!"

EP: That's an amazing story, partly because there's no way you can talk like that to police now without being confronted. I have this terrible habit where I thank cops. I got tackled once because a cop thought I was someone else, and, partly out of fear, I thanked him. I always feel like an asshole when I do it, too.

PK: I did the same thing (laughs) when they frisked me. They frisked the reporters because they didn't want the reporters to have guns in court.

EP: Was this for the Harvey Milk trial?

PK: Yeah.

EP: During that trial, you coined the phrase "The Twinkie Defense," You've done this a couple of times, creating an expression or a term, that becomes a permanent part of the language.

PK: I once started a list: Yippies, Twinkie Defense, jilling off — that's a woman masturbating, instead of jacking off.

EP: "Soft-core porn," you coined that.

PK: Yes.

EP: What do you think Robert Anton Wilson would say about Trump?

PK: He would be very analytical about him. You know, he would talk about the insanity of it. He would just get to the core of Trump. He'd be fascinated by it.

EP: He does like "mind fuckers."

PK: Exactly, yeah. He would be a great analyst of how we all have some narcissism in us, but Trump is the king of — oh, you know I'm doing now what you did — when you made up what you think what I would have said, there. And now I'm saying what Robert ... what Bob Wilson would say.

EP: But that's totally correct, I think.

PK: But he would, because — there was a European order of priests who got married, or something like that. And I gave Bob the assignment of writing about that convention of the priests, as if he was there. He loved doing that; he made it seem real.

That was a very good form of his satire, because once again, it was not *only* possible, it was probable.

EP: What about Terry Southern? A lot of people see *The Magic Christian* happening right now with Trump — Trump is living out that description of the book. He's "making it hot for them."

PK: Terry Southern was — he put a lot of words in italics when he wrote. And he talked the same way. He talked with italics.

EP: Maybe he'd italicize Trump. Finally, how do you think George Carlin would respond to Trump?

PK: He might make a list. George loved to make lists. He could make a list of lies, of Trump's lies.

EP: Paul, this has been so good talking with you. Any closing advice to Donald Trump, if he's reading?

PK: I got my philosophy from [the comic strip] *Mary Worth*: "When in doubt, do the kindest thing." **B**

VOL. 1, NO. 4 • SPRING 2017

Marvy

Ceci n'est pas une comic

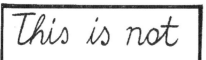

This is not

a pipe.

This is not

dangerous.

This is not

necessary.

This is not

your concern.

This is not

a problem.

This is not

a fascist.

with apologies to Magritte

Peter Kuper

WHEELER • FINCK • POND • HENDERSON • CRUSE • SLOAN • GAMMILL • KOFORD

CAMP MICRO-PENIS

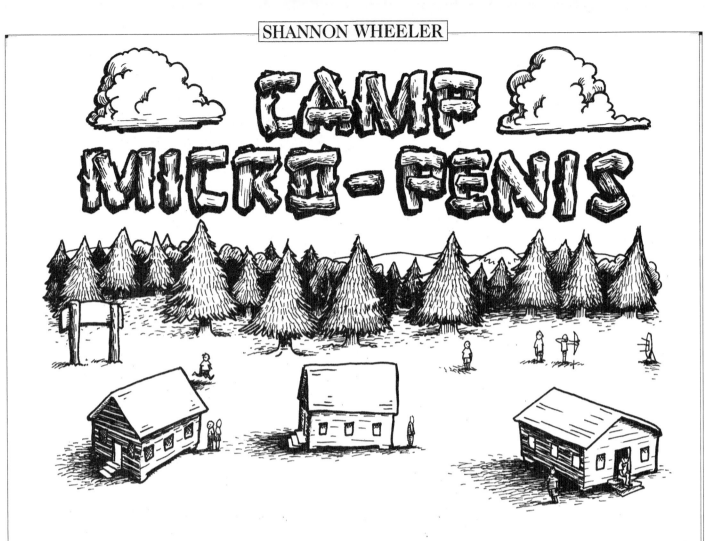

SHANNON WHEELER

I LOVED CAMP. IT WAS *TWO WEEKS* OF TAKING CARE OF ANIMALS, HORSEBACK RIDING, MAKING ART, DOING SKITS, AND SWIMMING.

HAVE FUN!

OK.

ONE YEAR, THERE WAS A KID WHO HAD A *SUPER TINY PENIS.* WE ALL KNEW ABOUT IT BUT WE DIDN'T TALK ABOUT IT.

HEY!

HI!

IT WAS SMALLER THAN A *VIENNA SAUSAGE.*

MOST OF US WERE *PRE-PUBERTY*. A COUPLE KIDS WERE STARTING TO GROW A *LITTLE HAIR*.

I DIDN'T LIKE THE *COMMUNAL SHOWER*. I'D USUALLY WAIT FOR IT TO CLEAR OUT TO TAKE MY TURN.

WHEN I HEARD *LAUGHTER* COMING FROM THE STALL I KNEW *SOMETHING* WAS *WRONG*.

HA HA HA HA HA HA HA HA HA

THEY'RE MAKING FUN OF THE KID WITH THE *TURTLE DICK*.

I'D WATCHED A LOT OF *TELEVISION*. I *KNEW* WHAT I *HAD* TO DO.

I'M GOING TO HAVE TO *FIGHT THEM*.

...THERE WOULD BE A *FIGHT*. I'D LOSE UNTIL THE *LAST SECOND*. I'D LAND A *LUCKY PUNCH* AND *WIN*. EVERYONE WOULD BE *SORRY*. WE'D LEARN A *LIFE LESSON*. I'D EARN THE *RESPECT* OF MY *PEERS*. WE'D BECOME *FRIENDS*. MOST IMPORTANTLY, I'D MAKE THE BULLIES BECOME *BETTER PEOPLE*.

IN *REALITY*, THE *STRESS* GOT TO ME *LONG BEFORE* ANY FIGHT STARTED.

WHY AM I BAWLING? NOTHING HAS EVEN HAPPENED YET.

I WALKED TO THE SHOWERS EXPECTING THE *WORST*. WHAT I SAW MADE *NO SENSE*.

HE WAS LAUGHING *TOO*. THEY WEREN'T MAKING FUN OF HIM. THEY WERE *COMMISERATING*.

HE EVEN HAD A TINY *ERECTION*. IT WAS *SAD*. SEEING HIM LAUGH MADE MY HEAD *HURT*. HE WAS DEALING WITH HIS PROBLEM WITH *HUMOR, DIGNITY,* AND *GRACE*. I WAS IN *AWE*.

THE *BULLIES* WEREN'T BULLIES AT ALL. THEY HAD ACTUALLY *HELPED* HIM.

HE *HELPED* US TOO. WE WOULD *NEVER* BE INSECURE ABOUT THE SIZE OF OUR OWN *PENISES*. OUR PROBLEMS WERE *NOTHING* COMPARED TO WHAT HE WAS DEALING WITH. HE TOOK OUR *BURDEN*. HE WAS A PENIS

HE WAS OUR *PENIS MARTYR*. I WILL *NEVER* FORGET HIM

SOMEONE ELSE'S MITOCHONDRIA

"CHILDREN BORN THROUGH 'THREE-PERSON IVF' WOULD CONTAIN GENETIC MATERIAL FROM THREE PEOPLE." — THE BBC

 — FOR MY MOM —

FIGURE 1.
MITOCHONDRIA, THE TINY "POWERHOUSES OF THE CELL," IN THEIR NATURAL HABITAT.

CLARA AND DUANE ROBINSON HAD BEEN TRYING TO CONCEIVE FOR MANY YEARS, WITH NO LUCK. THEY GOT A SERIES OF GENETIC TESTS AND FOUND OUT THAT CLARA WAS THE CARRIER OF A RARE MITOCHONDRIAL DISORDER THAT WAS BEING TRANSFERRED TO THE EMBRYOS AND CAUSING THEM TO DIE.

SOME FACTS:

MITOCHONDRIA ARE PASSED DOWN FROM MOTHER TO CHILD.

THE MITOCHONDRIA GENERATE THE CELL'S ENERGY, SO A MITOCHONDRIAL DISORDER IS A SERIOUS THING, OFTEN FATAL.

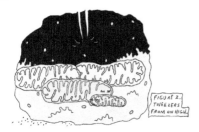

FIGURE 2.
TWEEZERS FROM ON HIGH.

FERTILITY DOCTORS CREATED AN EMBRYO FROM CLARA'S EGG AND DUANE'S SPERM USING IN VITRO FERTILISATION. THEY ALSO MADE ANOTHER EMBRYO FROM DUANE'S SPERM AND THE EGG OF AN ANONYMOUS DONOR. THE NUCLEUS OF THE SECOND EGG WAS REMOVED, LEAVING ONLY MITOCHONDRIA. THESE WERE TO BE HARVESTED (FIGURE 3).

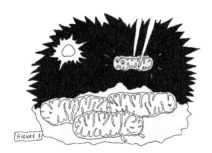

FIGURE 3

NINE MONTHS LATER, CANDICE ROBINSON WAS BORN, HEALTHY AND RADIATING WITH ENERGY.

INSET: THE MITOCHONDRION IS THE POWERHOUSE OF THE CELL.

FIGURE 4. THE JOY OF HUMAN REPRODUCTION.

WHILE THEY WERE WRITING INVITATIONS FOR CANDICE'S BABY PARTY, CLARA AND DUANE LOST SLEEP OVER WHETHER TO INVITE THE ANONYMOUS DONOR. THEY FINALLY DECIDED NOT TO. ISN'T THAT THE POINT OF AN ANONYMOUS DONOR, THAT SHE HOLDS NO CLAIM ON YOU? STILL, THEY WORRIED.

FIGURE 5.
NORMALLY, MITOCHONDRIA ARE PASSED DOWN FROM MOTHER TO CHILD.

CLARA AND DUANE CHOSE THEIR GUESTS CAREFULLY. THEY WANTED NICE, CHEERFUL PEOPLE WHO WOULD BESTOW CANDICE WITH UNCOMPLICATED GIFTS, LIKE AVERAGE-TO-GOOD LOOKS AND AN APTITUDE FOR MATH. THEY DECIDED TO INVITE PEOPLE FROM THE NEIGHBORHOOD: THE JOHNSONS, THE WILSONS, THE THOMPSONS, THE SMITHS.

THE PARTY WAS GOING NICELY: THE CAKE HAD BEEN EATEN, AND BABY CANDICE HAD BEEN GIVEN THE GIFTS OF SMARTNESS, LOOKS AND A LOYAL HEART. MR. AND MRS. SMITH WERE JUST ABOUT TO ENDOW HER WITH A SUNNY PERSONALITY—WHEN THE FRONT DOOR BLEW OPEN AND IN MARCHED THE ANONYMOUS DONOR. THE ROOM FELL SILENT.

"I HAVE ALREADY GIVEN CANDICE A GIFT," SAID THE DONOR. "I HAVE GIVEN HER THE GIFT OF MITOCHONDRIA. BUT SINCE A DONOR IS BY NATURE GENEROUS, I WILL ALSO GIVE HER ANOTHER SMALL GIFT. HERE IT IS: I WILL ALWAYS BE BY CANDICE'S SIDE, BUT WHEN SHE NEEDS ME MOST, SHE WILL BE UNABLE TO SEE ME. LONELINESS WILL GIVE HER POWER, AND HER ATTEMPTS TO CONTACT ME WILL HELP HER FIND HER TRUE VOICE.

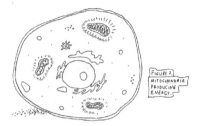

FIGURE 7. MITOCHONDRIA PRODUCING ENERGY.

CANDICE'S DISPOSITION COULD NOT BE CALLED SUNNY. SHE WAS A SERIOUS CHILD. FROM A VERY EARLY AGE, SHE WAS AWARE OF HER THIRD PARENT HOVERING QUIETLY IN THE BACKGROUND. A COMFORTING PRESENCE THAT NONETHELESS SET CANDICE APART. SOMETIMES SHE WOULD OPEN HER LUNCHBOX AND FIND A SURPRISE INSIDE: A TINY POTTED PLANT, FOR INSTANCE, A TYPE OF PLANT THAT DID NOT GROW WHERE SHE LIVED.

FIGURE 8. "PASSED DOWN FROM MOTHER TO CHILD."

ONCE IN AWHILE, CANDICE WOULD OPEN HER CLOSET — WHICH CLARA HAD MADE SURE TO STOCK WITH THE RIGHT KINDS OF JEANS AND SWEATERS — AND WOULD FIND ONLY OUTLANDISH COSTUMES FROM ANOTHER TIME AND PLACE. SHE ALWAYS WORE THEM, DESPITE HER PARENTS' CONCERNED GLANCES.

MOST PEOPLE WOULD CONSIDER A THIRD PARENT TO BE A BURDEN, BUT TO CANDICE, WHO NEVER QUITE FIT IN IN HER HOMETOWN, THE ANONYMOUS DONOR WAS A GREAT COMFORT. SHE KNEW TO KEEP THE ANONYMOUS DONOR'S PRESENCE TO HERSELF. CLARA AND DUANE WERE GOOD PEOPLE, BUT NOT FANCIFUL, AND THE KIDS AT SCHOOL WERE NEITHER FANCIFUL NOR GOOD.

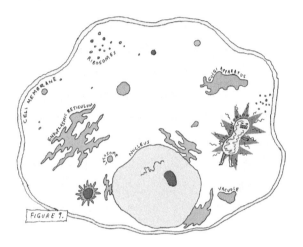

MEANWHILE, INSIDE CANDICE'S CELLS, THE MITOCHONDRION IS ALWAYS THE ODD ONE OUT. IT PRODUCES ENERGY, AS IT SHOULD — BUT THE ENERGY IT PRODUCES IS SOMEHOW FOREIGN.

FIGURE 9.

AT CELL PARTIES, IT IS ALWAYS THE MITOCHONDRION WHO GETS DRUNK AND TRIES TO MAKE OUT WITH THE NUCLEUS.

MITOCHONDRION

NUCLEUS

IT HANGS PHOTOGRAPHS OF ITS HOME COUNTRY ON THE CELL MEMBRANE. HOMESICKNESS WAFTS OFF THE MITOCHONDRION LIKE STEAM OFF HOT PAVEMENT.

FIGURE 10

MOSTLY, THE MITOCHONDRION JUST BIDES ITS TIME, THINKING THAT ONE DAY IT WILL FIND AN OUTLET FOR ITS STRANGE ENERGY.

AS CANDICE GREW UP, THE ANONYMOUS DONOR REMAINED IN THE BACKGROUND, APPEARING NOW AND THEN TO GIVE HER SMALL PRESENTS —

AND THE OCCASIONAL, PRECIOUS PIECE OF ADVICE.

MOSTLY, THOUGH, THE ANONYMOUS DONOR WAS SIMPLY, QUIETLY "THERE." THEN, ON CANDICE'S SEVENTEENTH BIRTHDAY, SHE CAME OUT WITH A SURPRISINGLY GRANDIOSE IDEA: "YOU'VE NEVER BELONGED IN THIS TOWN," SAID THE DONOR MATTER-OF-FACTLY. "YOU NEED TO LEAVE AND FIND YOUR PEOPLE."

"WHO ARE MY PEOPLE?" ASKED CANDICE. "YOUR PEOPLE ARE ANONYMOUS," SAID THE DONOR.

CANDICE'S PARENTS TEARED UP A LITTLE WHEN SHE LEFT FOR COLLEGE. THEY BROUGHT HER TO THE AIRPORT AND HUGGED HER GOODBYE. "DON'T FORGET WHERE YOU CAME FROM," THEY SAID. BUT AS THE PLANE LIFTED OFF, CANDICE'S OLD LIFE — THE RIGHT JEANS AND SWEATERS, PARABOLAS, THE WAR OF 1812, "THE MITOCHONDRION IS THE POWERHOUSE OF THE CELL" — SHRANK TO A SPECK AND DISAPPEARED.

SHE THOUGHT ABOUT "HER PEOPLE," WHOM SHE WAS SOON TO MEET. THINGS WERE ABOUT TO CHANGE FOR HER.

WHEN CLASSES STARTED, CANDICE HAD THREE REVELATIONS IN QUICK SUCCESSION. THE FIRST WAS THAT SHE WASN'T GOING TO START FITTING IN, THERE, OR ANYWHERE. SHE WAS A GENETIC ANOMALY — THE ONLY GIRL IN THE WORLD WITH THREE PARENTS. IT WAS HER FATE TO BE SET APART FROM OTHERS.

THE SECOND REVELATION WAS THAT SHE DIDN'T MIND BEING SET APART.

SHE WAS GRIPPED BY A SUDDEN SENSE OF URGENCY AND HURRIED BACK TO HER DORM ROOM TO TELL THE ANONYMOUS DONOR FOR THE FIRST TIME HOW GRATEFUL SHE WAS, FOR EVERYTHING.

BUT THE ANONYMOUS DONOR WAS GONE. THAT WAS THE THIRD REVELATION.

SCIENTISTS ASSURE US THAT CHILDREN BORN THROUGH THREE-PERSON IVF ARE NO DIFFERENT THAN OTHER CHILDREN. AN ANONYMOUS DONOR IS A HELPFUL STRANGER, NOTHING MORE.

THERE ARE SEVERAL WAYS TO CREATE A HUMAN. THERE IS SEX. THERE IS SCIENCE. ALSO, SOMETIMES, WHEN SOMEONE IS EXTREMELY LONELY, SHE MAY CREATE A FRIEND OR A PARENT OUT OF THIN AIR.

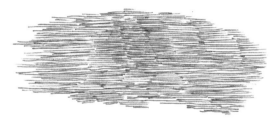

FOR THE FIRST TIME, CANDICE REALLY TOOK STOCK OF HER SURROUNDINGS. SHE WAS ALONE. THERE WAS A PEN ON THE TABLE. INSIDE CANDICE'S CELLS, SOMETHING BEGAN, JOYOUSLY, TO SPIN.

FIGURE 11.

"THREE-PERSON IVF" WAS PRACTICED SUCCESSFULLY IN THE LATE 1990'S AND EARLY 2000'S AND WAS LATER BANNED BECAUSE OF THE ETHICAL QUESTIONS IT RAISES. THE PROCEDURE IS STILL ILLEGAL IN THE U.S., BUT THE U.K. IS PLANNING TO LEGALIZE IT THIS YEAR.

B

MiDLiFe CRiSiS Cliches of the UNHiP and the HiP

...ACQUIRES SPORTSCAR.

...ACQUIRES VINTAGE CAR.

...GETS PLASTIC SURGERY.

...GETS VINTAGE PLASTIC CLOTHING.

...DEVELOPS CRUSH ON YOUNG SECRETARY.

...DEVELOPS CRUSH ON YOUNG BARISTA.

(continued)

...SUFFERS EXISTENTIAL ANGST.

...SUFFERS EXISTENTIAL ANGST.

...BUYS NEW LEATHER JACKET.

...BUYS OLD LEATHER JACKET.

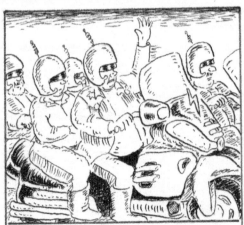

...JOINS MOTORCYCLE CLUB FILLED WITH OTHER AGING NONHIPSTERS, DOESN'T REALIZE HOW PATHETIC THIS IS.

...TRIES TO JOIN REAL MOTORCYCLE CLUB. ALMOST GETS KILLED. FEELS YOUNG AGAIN.

LOOSE PAGES

1996

COME HERE, LET ME TELL YOU THE DIFFERENCE BETWEEN CATS AND DOGS!

BAH, I'LL NEVER NEED TO KNOW THAT!

YOU'D THINK HE'D FIGURE OUT THE FOURTH TIME THAT ANONYMOUS SEX ADS ON CRAIG'S LIST ARE USUALLY BEES IN THE SHAPE OF A PERSON!

2016

WHAT IS THAT? IF ONLY I'D PAID ATTENTION TO THAT GUY TWENTY YEARS AGO!

LOOK AT THAT ANIMAL!

WHAT A NICE PET!

WE WANT YOUZE TO PUT JOEY CALZONE IN YOUR NEXT PICTURE, OR ELSE!

I JUST MAKE VIDEOS OF SQUIRRELS WATERSKIING ON YOUTUBE! HOW CAN I FIT HIM? YOU'RE WASTING YOUR TIME!

YOU'LL FIGURE IT OUT!

THE NEXT MORNING...

≡YAWN≡

AA

IT WAS FUNNY WHEN I THOUGHT OF IT! THE IDEA WAS HE'D WAKE UP AND HIS BED WAS FILLED WITH SQUIRREL HEADS BUT I THOUGHT IT MIGHT BOTH BE TOO GRUESOME AND TOO UNFUNNY AT THE SAME TIME. IT SEEMED REALLY FUNNY BEFORE I DREW IT. SORRY.

@henderson17

150 years ago in AMERICAN BYSTANDER

THE AMERICAN BYSTANDER
CAVALCADE OF DROLLERY, WHIMSY AND ASSORTED COMMENTARIES

HE (to SHE): "I shall have a bright future as a cobbler provided I am not fined too many shillings should a wandering minstrel ask for pointy shoes rather than the piked ones currently in fashion."

HORRIBLE HUSBANDS OF MANY LANDS

SPAIN

MAKE ME A PAELLA!

VIETNAM

MAKE ME A BAHN MI!

FRANCE

MAKE ME ESCARGOTS AUX FINES HERBES!

CANADA

B

Brother Worm's Revelation by Howard Cruse

Zen of Nimbus

by Michael Sloan

The Doozies

by Tom Gammill

ADAM KOFORD

COMPLETE ENCYCLOPEDIA SET

MATCHBOOK

PENCIL SET

UKULELE BOOK

LOCK PICK SET

1937 CALENDAR

3 ICE CREAM SANDWICHES

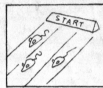
MOUSE RACE SET

POLYGRAPH

MISMATCHED SOCKS

BONFIRE KIT

BASEBALL CARDS

PASSPORT SET

CHEMISTRY SET

COUNTERFEIT MONEY

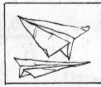
PAPER AIRPLANES

CANDY CIGARETTES

FILE SET

HAUNTED LOCKET

ADVANCED SHIV

BASKETBALL & HOOP

"I sell American seeds on death row."
Joel Bellhop
Ossining, New York

"It's an easy way to get money in prison."
Martha Zimmerman
Marion, Illinois

"I stayed in prison so I could keep selling."
William Zilliam
Polunsky, Texas

MAKE MONEY IN PRISON
with Fast Selling American Seeds

Take your choice of 700 contraband prizes. You can earn as many as you can hide. All prizes shown here and many more in our Big Prize Book are given AT GREAT COST for selling just one 300 pack order of Prisoner's Vegetable and Flower Seeds at 20¢ a year. Some of the larger prizes require more information before they can be revealed.

Send MONEY, we do not trust you

Every prisoner wants a variety of seeds, fresh and ready to grow. You'll sell them quickly to wardens, trustys, cellmates, and guards. Many boys and girls sell their packs in one day. You can too, and then choose your prize or take the cash (upon release from prison). Good luck.

USE THESE COUPONS ONLY

To order your seeds, fill out one of these coupons and hand it to your warden.

PRISONERS SEED CO.
Block 946
Leavenworth, KANSAS
Here for life...

SCRIBBLIA   STAIN PODS
HAM   STINKO
SPORES   POP CORN
DIRT CLODS

EXTRA!

$3,000 REWARD GIVEN for information leading to the capture & arrest of notorious seed thieves.

We will catch you sooner or later, you miscreant(s)!

HELP US LOCK UP THESE CRIMINALS

SEEDS   SEEDS

MAIL ONE COUPON TODAY!
Give the other to your cellmate

PRISONERS SEED CO. BLOCK 946, LEAVENWORTH, KANSAS
Please send me your illustrated instruction book on how to sell seeds in prison. I will sell them at 20¢ per pack or face an extension of my sentence.

☐ Warden's initials   ☐ Attorney/family approval

Name _____

Prison _____

Sentence _____ Last meal _____

PRISONERS SEED CO. BLOCK 946, LEAVENWORTH, KANSAS
Please send me your illustrated instruction book on how to sell seeds in prison. I will sell them at 20¢ per pack or face an extension of my sentence.

☐ Warden's initials   ☐ Attorney/family approval

Name _____

Prison _____

Sentence _____ Last meal _____

ROADSIDE AMERICANS

Roger Babson battled two things: moral decay, and gravity. Roger Babson lost • By Mike Wilkins

If you ever find yourself stumbling down a certain ill-marked, half-overgrown path in the chill and barren woods near Gloucester, Massachusetts, two questions are likely to be top-of-mind: *Where did my life go so wrong?* and *Why does that rock have "Help Mother" carved on it?*

The first one is unanswerable. The second has a tale behind it.

Roger Babson grew up in Gloucester, and attended MIT in the 1890s. Soon after graduation, he started Babson's Statistical Organization, a pioneer in providing organized and reliable market and economic data to a burgeoning Wall Street. He became a rich young man applying Sir Isaac Newton's principles of motion to the stock market.

After the panic of 1907, Babson started giving financial advice to the public; for decades, he was a regular columnist for *The New York Times* and *The Saturday Evening Post*. In September 1929, he predicted October's famous market meltdown: "A crash is coming, and it may be terrific...The vicious circle will get in full swing and the result will be a serious business depression."

Tycoon Roger Babson in 1918, before he got a little intense.

conditions; his secretaries were issued blankets and metal claws to type dictation during the cold Massachusetts winters.

Odd as he was, Babson was also intensely public-spirited, and occasionally did some real good. After witnessing the effects of fire on crowded slums, for example, he took control of a company that would create America's iconic street corner fire alarm, the Gamewell Masterbox. He believed in public sanitation, and further fortune was made with a company that manufactured and sold paper towel dispensers, now ubiquitous in public restrooms.

Babson's vision of the good life was simple: "normal sex relations, playing with little children, and a good meal after a hard day's work." How to get there? One should develop the skin to resist variations in temperature by means of cold baths, massage and vigorous rubbing with paper towels, the kind ubiquitously dispensed by his machines. And as with every thinker of this type, his thoughts inevitably strayed into the bathroom: Babson swore by three good bowel movements each day and a mild laxative every Saturday night, whether you needed it or not.

A MAN OF ACTION

Already Babson was a quintessential American type: a self-made, well-heeled eccentric, using vast resources to communicate prescriptions for a life well-lived. Some of his activities were the typical prerogatives of wealth: He founded colleges[1], ran for president in 1940 on the Prohibition ticket, and authored more than 50 books. Other schemes were more unconventional — for Babson was the kind of polymath who had an answer for everything, regardless of where the trail of logical breadcrumbs took him. When nearly felled by tuberculosis, he decided indoor germs were the cause and subsequently worked outside regardless of

HIS PIECE OF THE ROCK

In Babson's eyes, the Great Depression was primarily a moral condition worsened by the repeal of Prohibition, and needed to be tackled at all points along the front. So at the same time he was advising Presidents Hoover and Roosevelt, and publishing his book, *Cheer Up!*, he also donated to Gloucester 500 acres of scrub, then started carving uplifting aphorisms on its large, jutting rocks.

In part this was an act of charity, make-work for the unemployed stonecutters of Gloucester; but it was also Edwardian Bootstrap Gospel in physical form. "My family says that I am defacing the boulders and disgracing the family," Babson wrote. "I am really trying to write a simple book with words carved in stone instead of printed paper." Sev-

---

[1] In addition to Babson College and Webber College, both of which still exist in some form, he founded the unforgettably named Utopia College, a novelty sweatshirt waiting to happen.

eral dozen "Babson Boulders" remain today broadcasting their motivational messages to rabbits, deer, and the occasional lost hiker. "If Work Stops, Values Decay"; "Never Try, Never Win"; "Keep Out of Debt"; "Use Your Head"; "Be Clean"; "Help Mother"; "Prosperity Follows Service"; and, perhaps inevitably, "Get A Job."

But woodland creatures are as feckless as they are illiterate, and Babson's slogans do not seem to have inspired many humans, either. The scrubland has overgrown into genuine woods. Trees have sprouted and largely reclaimed the rocks, and to find them at all, one must stroll down some ill-marked and near-empty paths. The rocks are further down the path than you might expect, and the ruggedness and solitude give the place its incongruous charm.

"THAT DRAGON GRAVITY"

The civic-minded, gently lunatic tycoon took one final stab at immortality. When his 13-year-old sister Edith died from drowning in 1893, the culprit was clear to Babson. And in 1947 when his grandson drowned, also taken by "that dragon gravity," enough was enough. So at age 73, Babson founded the Gravity Research Foundation. He put the headquarters in New Boston, New Hampshire, after determining that this location was far enough away from Boston, Massachusetts, to survive a nuclear attack on the bigger city. The essay written to announce the foundation was entitled, "Gravity – Our Enemy Number One." Pamphlets were published like "Gravity and Posture," "Gravity and the Weather" and "Gravity and Your Feet." Gravity had its talons in everything, from "the common cold, house fires,

the firing of General Douglas MacArthur and hemorrhoids."

Unfortunately, Americans were as cold to the dangers of gravity as they'd been to Babson's aphorisms in granite. After a fruitless decade of unheeded warnings, the businessman changed tack; he decided to donate money to colleges, to inspire the gravity researchers of tomorrow on the condition that they place a special stone marker somewhere on campus to let students know about the opportunity. Beginning in 1960, more than a dozen took him up on the offer, including leading institutions like Colby, Middlebury and Tuskegee.[2] Solid granite and weighing more than a ton (at least until gravity is solved), they were placed "to remind students of the blessings forthcoming when a semi-insulator is discovered in order to harness gravity as a free power and reduce airplane accidents."

Fifty years later, these markers are treated with various degrees of seriousness and embarrassment. Gordon College used to hide theirs in a bush, and Emory put theirs in storage (until students successfully lobbied for its return). But Tufts displays theirs in President's Lawn, and cosmology graduates kneel at the stone while a professor drops an apple on their head.

When Roger Babson died in 1967, no more monuments were made and gravity continues, unimpeded. **B**

///////////////////////////////////////

Babson College, Babson Park, MA; Bethune-Cookman College, Daytona Beach, FL; Colby College, Waterville, ME; Eastern Baptist College, St. Davids, PA; Eastern Nazarene College, Quincy, MA; Emory University, Atlanta, GA; Gordon College, Wenham, MA; Hobart and William Smith Colleges, Geneva, NY; Keene State College, Keene, NH; Middlebury College, Middlebury, VT; Tufts University, Medford, MA; Tuskegee Institute, Tuskegee, AL; University of Tampa, Tampa, FL; and Wheaton College, Wheaton, IL.

Who needs high school guidance counselors when you have Babson boulders?

ASK A BYSTANDER!

High school reunion si or no, and the fate of good people • By Merrill Markoe

Dear Merrill: *Against my better judgment, I'm considering dragging my husband to my 25th high-school reunion. What makes this a particularly bad idea is that an old boyfriend (with whom I'm friendly on Facebook) is likely to be there.*

This has catastrophe written all over it, I know that, but I'm having a hard time talking myself out of it. Help!

An excellent question. The answer is complex because the online world in which we live seems to be divided into two important sectors: 1) people who love the idea of getting together with everyone from their past 2) me.

Even before I lived online, I avoided every high school reunion, happily turning a blind eye to invitations meant to flood me with thoughts of good times to be had with the grayer, fatter versions of the same people who used to give me stomach aches when I passed them in the halls.

When I was a teenager, I couldn't wait to graduate high school because, believe it or not, I attended back in those fanciful fairytale-like years when America was still coasting on its original greatness. By the way, all that greatness can now be traced to a single long-faded premise: how easy it was for people to lose track of one another.

Because I came of age before social media, I knew from the moment I first put up a website I was opening the door to a degree of intrusive discomfort. However, much to my surprise, it took me almost no time at all to develop the

MERRILL MARKOE is a Person of Infinite Empathy for *The American Bystander*.

numbness to pummeling required for assimilation into Facebook, *et al*. After an initial nearly lethal Orwellian adjustment, it all became relatively painless, reminiscent of the way the body learns to process common but alarming food additives known to cause cancer in lab rats only *some* of the time.

This brings us to Phase Two of online adjustment: a complete revamping of all the outdated ideas regarding common sense. You probably don't even remember the first time you succumbed to the pressure to regularly share something personal with a group of voracious strangers, knowing in your heart you had nothing worth sharing. Everyone gets used to it so quickly they barely notice the moment when daily life itself becomes a ritual to endure in order to score sufficiently interesting things to post online. Soon you've given a hearty thumbs-up to the idea of hosting a multimedia tour through a cuted-up thumbnail-sized museum of your daily life.

This brings us to the thorny ethical question lurking at the heart of all online life, also known as Phase Three.

Having offered up photos/videos of the flaky golden-crusted pumpkin coconut curry pie you made for dinner to the hundreds of bored strangers you've agreed to refer to as "Friends" — and accepted their "Likes" as a boost to your status — are you now obliged to schedule a time to meet face-to-face with them all? What if they write you a very very nice note and request a meeting? What if they write you another note after that, then another one? And If the answer is yes, you must meet them, do the same rules apply if the proposed social outing involves a person with whom you used to be intimate?

After all, when you insert the word ex-boyfriend or ex-girlfriend into the scenario, isn't it safe to assume that the reason you've been out of touch all

these decades is because the relationship went rancid at some point? Consider the specifics: Do you really want to commit to cleaning the house, setting the table, buying fresh flowers, worrying about what to wear, maybe even getting a haircut, then preparing a selection of smart little hors d'oeuvres and frosty iced beverages for an old boyfriend from high school who once wrote you a letter that said, "My love for you is dead"?

Come on! How in the world are you supposed to make small talk with this guy's adorable, probably very patient wife and at the same time show interest in their vacations and/or their children without disappearing into the quicksand of the long-buried memories connected to the horrible stuff you replied in your letter of retaliation? Can you believe what a loose cannon you used to be? What was the deal on you anyway?

Let's say you agree to this reunion. How would your afternoon unfold in a best-case scenario? Would team former-couple spin colorful yarns from their days of youthful romance as the present-day long-suffering mates force themselves to appear amused? How long will you be able to stand looking at that thing they are both doing with their faces, which appears to be someplace between a smile and a grimace? Why would you or anyone want to live through an afternoon like this, unless you were doing research for a four-person play? (And even then, this premise has been so often exploited in theaters both large and small, on Broadway and off, that it instantly puts a playwright on shaky ground with reviewers.)

Perhaps I'm overthinking things. I've been known to do that. But I have so many unanswered questions on how this might play out. What assurance do we have that some protective protocol kicks in to help prevent the principals from launching into an anecdotal rehashing of

the Diary of Merrill Markoe   Sept. 30, 1962

TODAY there was a lot of integration trouble. James Meredith wanted to ENROLL at the University of Mississippi BUT THEY WOULDN'T LET HIM because he was NEGRO so he SUED and won a court order to get to enroll accompanied by the Natl Guard.
Governor Burnett of Miss. got SO UPSET he AIDED the rioting and got taken to court.

In other news, I hate my retainer. Who knows how long I'll have to wear it.??

Thats how things are shaping up. Not good.

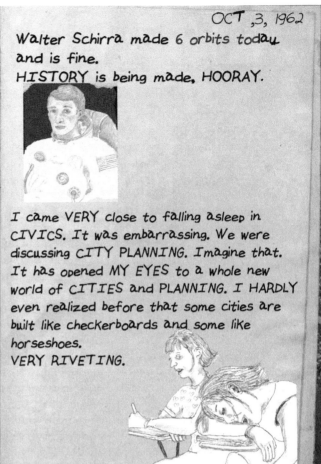

OCT, 3, 1962

Walter Schirra made 6 orbits today and is fine.
HISTORY is being made. HOORAY.

I came VERY close to falling asleep in CIVICS. It was embarrassing. We were discussing CITY PLANNING. Imagine that. It has opened MY EYES to a whole new world of CITIES and PLANNING. I HARDLY even realized before that some cities are built like checkerboards and some like horseshoes.
VERY RIVETING.

---

the worst of times? Or even worse, what if the sparks of magnetism from the early romantic days decide, against all odds, to re-emerge and become visible? What possible good could come of acquainting the present-day mates with any vision of a decades-old chemistry, especially one that has already proven itself to be a straight nonstop route to Mordor?

But moving beyond paranoia, let's imagine that the reunion, for some reason, goes well. Does this mean that the lucky foursome will all have to get together again and again? Because in that case, having used up the "A" material on this nerve-racking first occasion, what memories will be left to exploit for entertainment in the future? Won't they then have to settle for lamer, more mediocre anecdotes, as the ice they are skating on gets thinner and thinner, until they find themselves barely able to stay awake during a discussion of extended family and friends neither of them have had contact with in decades?

So there you all sit, nibbling on wasabi peas, trying to ignore the fact that you are just a semi-permeable membrane away from talking about some grisly, misery-soaked argument you have been trying to block for over 25 years. Wasn't everyone better off when all this stuff was sealed in an airtight space/time capsule deep inside the hippocampus or frontal cortex? At least in its original vintage form everyone looked a lot cuter.

Therefore, I am forced to conclude that when all is said and done, the only valid purpose of a reunion of this nature is to demonstrate what better choices everyone is making these days, with the payoff coming during the final fond fare-wells, as each couple quietly mumbles to themselves: "Ha! Can you believe I was stupid enough to have spent five years with THAT?" Which brings us back to my original question: Did you waste all this time and money buying brand-new placemats and making lovely spinach and feta cheese tartlets just to reassure yourself you took the right fork in the road? Or was it really to give everyone something festive to post on Facebook? (And by the way, the ex had better not try and post those damn pictures first.)

This has been a rather long-winded way of telling you: "No. Don't do it." Especially not during cold and flu season, when there are so many easy-to-fake symptoms available for free.

Ask yourself this: Why would you want to waste time reliving the melancholy of the past when you live in a world so full of dispiriting things in the present? Watch the news. Read Twitter. As long as Trump is president, there will always be misery in abundance. Open your heart and it will be yours.

Is any place in this world safe for intelligent people with big hearts?

Well, your best option is trying to convince Sir David Attenborough to adopt you. Failing that, consider taking Jane Goodall as your role model and relocating to the wild with a pack of endangered animals.

If neither of those work for you, the answer is no. No place is safe for intelligent people with big hearts. So find a new show to binge-watch. I suggest *The Good Wife.* B

P.S. MUELLER THINKS LIKE THIS

The cartoonist/broadcaster/writer is always walking around, looking at stuff • By P.S. Mueller

Possible Lagerfelds

Take a close look at Karl Lagerfeld. No, stop! He might take a close look back and start following you around, stalking you like a warm cyborg constructed of duck jerky and redolent of castrati musk. Unlike the rest of us, he may be powered by the tides. Were he to remove the shades, all within his range could burn like magnesium while dancing obliviously in million dollar shoes. Yet he may be also a good man, purposefully distracting despots and players from power, fame and genocide to transform them into harmless suckers like the rest of us.

Perhaps he will follow you home to meet the wife and kids. He will lift the lid on a pot of stew and sigh. Later on, that hairpiece, white as treated teeth, will come off, eight Budweisers will make their way to his wary heart, and the old man will dream on the old Naugahyde chair downstairs in the corner of the rec room. But you won't tell him about how that very same chair once captivated Ralph Lauren's chapped ass. Ralph Lauren stopped coming by when your Aunt Milly moved to Argentina upon learning of his bitter hatred of gauchos. You didn't like Ralph anyway, so no big deal. But it just may be, if Karl slips out of that impossible collar and tilts into free and easy chat with that

I DON'T BUY THE SCIENCE ON PANTS.

MUELLER

cutting-edge platinum ear trumpet of his, the old fellow turns out to be a different guy altogether. He might laugh and laugh and laugh about the time Anna Wintour clocked him with a genuine Tiffany lamp. And later, in the guest bedroom, a secret confession of abiding love for that guy on *Duck Dynasty*, the horrible one.

Nice thought anyway. But what if Karl Lagerfeld were to coldly observe that you are 65 and dress like a 10-year-old from 1961? What if he's a real self-made Bond villain with a right iron claw, a left platinum eye and the steely will to impose high fashion on the down-low? For all you know he has built his empire one customer at a time, terrorizing an innocent one percent through blackmail, kidnapping or cunningly simulated hurricane damage. After all, like it or not, you have been glimpsing him in print and on TV for decades, barely noticing as his ubiquitous brand relentlessly hardens like an unwanted chrysalis around your carelessly guarded Kevlar sense of self. But why? You are neither royalty nor rich. But you *did* take a close look, didn't you? Your eyes met, he saw those pleated

Dockers concealing your pleated ass and, and, that look you always fail to hide when you're assessing a grotesque. He's old and made of leather stuffed with bluebird feathers, but he is formidable. Word has it that if you can trick him into getting a blue rinse, he will set you free.

Then again, what if the man de-mummifies and reaches out to you with his real hand? But he's all tangled up in an experimental ascot, and out of pity you shoehorn it over his remarkable head with the help of extra virgin olive oil and a copy of *Vanity Fair*. There *is* some small part of you that wouldn't even want Bernie Madoff to die in an ascot, isn't there? And then suppose that Lagerfeld, to show his gratitude, invites you to his palace for dinner with billionaires. Will he watch you closely? Will he follow you to the servants' quarters, where you're always more comfortable eating with the help? Will he sit quietly — watching you through those opaque glasses while sipping something extracted from a swan, as you let it drop that, nice guy that he is and all, you consider his life's work to be a crime against reality? And what if the room goes quiet then and you take another close look at Karl Lagerfeld, just barely making out the whisper of his feeble request for decanted tears, directed to the butler staring a furious hole in in the back of your head?

Three-Second Movie

The redheaded girl was savage. She would take a hammer to a frog. Both of her parents were doctors.

• • •

Rome wasn't built in a day, but Schaumberg, Illinois, was.

P.S. MUELLER (@mgerber937) is Staff Liar of *The American Bystander*.

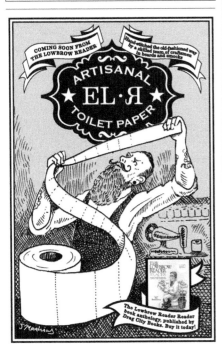
Dr. and Walter Parkay

"It says right here on the card that you are a pediatrician from Wooster, Ohio. Are you a liar, Mr. Parkay? Ten million people are looking on, Mr. Parkay. What do you say to them?"

So spoke John Charles — former star of the "Second Chance With Hair" series of infomercials and current host of the syndicated game show *Take a Guess*. His slab of outsized face was slowly turning the color of beet soup.

Charles clearly had it in for me from the moment his associate producer stepped across the set during a break; in whispered tones, Charles was informed that I was *not* the man described on the card. I wasn't *Doctor* Walter Parkay. But I was, and remain, Walter Parkay — the only other Walter Parkay on earth. I never lied to anyone.

It is obvious to me now that nobody involved with *Take A Guess* studied up on the good doctor's doings past 2011; that was the year he legally married his own vintage Mercury Montclair, and got famous. That's what Charles wanted to talk to me about. But in 2013, Dr. Parkay was arrested and charged with malpractice after being caught treating assorted serious childhood diseases with hominy. *Hominy, for God's sake!*

Anyway, if you're willing to drive aimlessly back and forth along Interstate 80 near Vacaville, California, anytime between now and 2021, *Doctor* Walter Parkay is easy to spot. He's the only member of his work gang wearing a white lab coat.

I, on the other hand, am an honest man, a hard-working blue-collar guy with a wife and kids. I handle a cutting torch at a guardrail factory in Illinois and just happened to be visiting a cousin in Anaheim when a nice young woman handed me tickets to *Take a Guess*.

Again, I make a safety product created for the sole purpose of preventing cars and trucks from colliding head-on. By the thousands. A noble and honorable way to spend one's life, to my way of thinking. No bizarre matrimony; no grits-based quackery. And when I told my cousin Phil I was going to be on *Take a Guess*, he researched the whole show for me, including John Charles.

This was my reply:

"Mr. Charles and fellow Americans, my first name is not 'Doctor.' Doctor Parkay is in prison where he belongs.

"Now I have a question for you, sir. Are you the same John Charles who agreed to pay an out-of-court settlement two years ago after being sued by numerous female employees of your program? Did they really accuse you of repeatedly asking them if you could 'Waldorf their salads'? Also, can you think about your answer while we go ahead and play *Take a Guess?*"

• • •

Oh to be a mindless dove
unconcerned with hopeless love
or wintry gods so far above,
I would give that chickadee a shove.

• • •

Plans are in the works for the Frito-Lay Corporation to market a new "All-Day Cheeto," priced for budget-minded consumers. Spokesmen at Frito-Lay say the 50-inch, 40-pound snack will come packaged in its own little jumpsuit.

• • •

Even Superman broke a few planets before he found the Earth.

• • •

Screen star Sylvester Stallone is undergoing a strict training program for his upcoming role as a burlap bag full of butter beans. However, rumors that the actor has also agreed to portray 200 pears in a silk track suit have been hotly denied by his agent.

Michael Bloomberg *Can* Jump

Though he's over 70 years of age, money mogul Michael Bloomberg is said to be nearly superhuman in terms of physical grace and stamina. In fact, Bloomberg is a legend on the private basketball courts of New York City, where CEOs and hedge-funders gather for some serious roundball.

Venture capitalist Bryce Wallet swears he once saw the former mayor climb Lloyd Blankfein like a meth-crazed chimp. And Bloomberg reputedly has a sky hook to beat them all as well, according to Super 8 motel magnate Jerry Super: "Sometimes all you can do is stand back and yell 'Look at that billionaire jump!'"

B

CHUNK-STYLE NUGGETS

...to briefly distract you from the inevitable • By Steve Young

"Remember, if your mouth develops wifi, blame a cherry, not a radioactive pea."

Horoscope for the Comatose

Sagittarius: You may be under pressure from family or friends to "change" or "try harder." Continue to ignore them.

Capricorn: You display an inability to finish what you started, but you're untroubled by it, and that's endearing.

Aquarius: All things considered, not an auspicious week for a career change. Relax and enjoy some "down time."

Pisces: You should be proud of the progress you've made lately in keeping your temper under control.

Aries: High-maintenance relationships are not in the stars right now. At this point in your life, you need unconditional love.

Taurus: Some people may consider you stubbornly self-centered, but the fact is that you're simply in a world of your own.

Gemini: You haven't been taking proper care of your finances lately. If you're not going to be proactive, accept help.

Cancer: Long periods of quiet contemplation may be good for the soul, but consider getting more exercise.

Leo: You crave being the center of attention, but it's not as easy as it used to be. Accept the fact that the spotlight has moved on.

STEVE YOUNG (@pantssteve) is Oracle for *The American Bystander*.

Virgo: There was a time when you would have been upset about being labeled "boring" or "predictable," but you're past that.

Libra: Others may be jealous of your serenity, but that's their problem, not yours. Remain above the fray.

Scorpio: They think you don't hear, but you're well aware of what's being said. Keep playing your long game.

Around This Date In History

A week ago Thursday was the 65 millionth anniversary of the asteroid strike that killed all dinosaurs with last names beginning with letters A through M.

Yesterday was the 39th birthday of that guy Ted you met at your last job who has that thing on his cheek.

Life Hacks!

Handy Conversion Table
1 tablespoon = 17 forkfuls of liquid
1 mile = 1.13 inaccurate miles
1 pound = too much cilantro

Mnemonic Device for Remembering the Name "Roy G. Biv"

Red, Orange, Yellow, Green, Blue, Indigo, Violet

Did you know? Mr. Biv's middle name is Gravlax, an old family name.

English Sentences To Practice Even If You're Already Fluent In English

1. "As a Director's Circle museum member, I am allowed to lick the paintings."
2. "Have you noticed a certain emotional reserve in some of Grandmother's tropical fish?"
3. "I'm sorry, the left-handed are not permitted on this Ferris wheel."

More Life Hacks!

Because it's better to be safe than sorry: Never leave home unless you're wearing a beekeeper outfit.

If You're on the International Space Station and One of Your Fellow Astronauts Develops Acute Appendicitis

1. **Secure patient** to work surface, anesthetize patient with syringe labeled "Emergency Anesthetic"

2. ***Carefully cut open*** patient's lower abdomen with sterilized scalpel, stanch bleeding with clamps

3. ***Locate the red, swollen appendix*** attached to lower large intestine, cut it off

4. ***Sew appendix stump*** shut with surgical needle and thread, repeat for abdominal incision

5. ***When patient dies*** several hours later, eject corpse (and appendix) through airlock, report to Mission Control that there's been a "tragic space walk accident."

Spotlight On...
A U.S. President Who Was Never Conceived Therefore Never Born Nor Elected

Thaddeus R. Tarbell

Thaddeus R. Tarbell would have been the 20th president, defeating James Garfield in the election of 1880, had his father and mother engaged in intercourse on the evening of June 5th, 1822, and conceived him. Unfortunately his father, Algernon, was ill that night due to eating tainted venison, and Thaddeus subsequently failed to exist. Had he been conceived, born and elected, President Tarbell would be remembered chiefly for being forced from office during the 1881 Steam Corset Scandal.

Invention Applications Recently Rejected by the U.S. Patent Office

Olive re-pitter
Glow-in-the-dark novelty surgical stents
Sewn fabric "case for a pillow"
1975 Chevrolet Malibu
Facial non-recognition software
Whale-oil-powered clock radio
Combination mail collection box/shredder
Casket on skis
Alphabet soup with umlauts

Match Each Animal With Its Email Address!

 Jeff9668@yahoo.com

 Seth855@hotmail.com

 Jeff1144@hotmail.com

 Geof297@hotmail.com

 BootyLover12@yahoo.com

 Seth7471@hotmail.com

Answers on p. 91 of some other publication.

Spoiler Alert
The sun eventually becomes a "red giant" and engulfs the Earth, extinguishing all life. **B**

GIMME THE GOOD STUFF

The best classic (pre-2000) comedy in every medium, according to our staff. Updated regularly.

Books

Advanced Cartooning (AK)
Barefoot Boy With Cheek (MW)
The Beast of Monsieur Racine (MSl)
The Benchley Roundup (DC, MG, MM, JMT)
Bill the Galatic Hero (JAW)
Bored of the Rings (MG)
Catch-22 (4x)
Cat's Cradle (JG)
A Century of College Humor (MG)
Cloudland Revisited (AJ)
A Confederacy of Dunces (LS, DV)
The Curse of Lono (NS)
Decline and Fall (DV)
Dirk Gently's Holistic Detective Agency (BO)
Dog of the South (RC, MR)
Don Martin Steps Out (PM)
The Fran Lebowitz Reader (JMT)
Getting Even (MRe, DV)
A Handful of Dust (TJ)
Hellbent On Insanity (MG)
I Am Blind and My Dog Is Dead (KK)
The Illustrated Boys' Own (MG)
In God We Trust, All Others Pay Cash (MG)
Jailbird (BO)
The Last Laugh (ND)
The Lazlo Letters (JH, MO)
Lucky Jim (JP)

The Magic Ghristian (JR)
Master and Margarita (TJ)
My Brother Was an Only Child (RG)
My World and Welcome to It (BMc)
Naked (BO)
Naked Pictures of Famous People (JMT)
The National Lampoon Tenth Anniversary Anthology (MG, JO)
The National Lampoon High School Yearbook Parody (4x)
Norwood (RC, RS)
Portnoy's Complaint (JR)
The Portable Dorothy Parker (MM)
Science Made Stupid (AK)

Side Effects (JMT, DV)
The Sot-Weed Factor (DL)
Stern (RC, JZ)
Stiff Upper Lip, Jeeves (MO)
Stuff and Nonsense (BKT)
Surely You're Joking, Mr. Feynman! (BO)
The Thirteen Clocks (BO)
What Happens Next? (JR)
Wise Blood (TJ)
Without Feathers (JO, DV)
Women — Bukowski (KS)
Zany Afternoons (SY)

LPs

A Star Is Bought (TG)
Bicenntennial Nigger (MG)
The Button-Down Mind of Bob

Newhart (JMT)
Bring the Pain (JR)
Class Clown (LS)
The Day the Laughter Died (JR)
Derek & Clive: Come Again — Peter Cook and Dudley Moore (MO)
Derek & Clive: The Worst Job I Ever Had — Peter Cook and Dudley Moore (KK)
"I used to love listening to Cosby albums, but that experience is now gone" (JMT)
Don't Crush That Dwarf, Hand Me the Pliers (RS)
Eddie Murphy (NS)
How Can You Be in Two Places at Once When You're Not Anywhere at All? (JG)
I Put a Spell on You—Nina Simone (KS)
Inside Shelly Berman (JB)
...Is It Something I Said? (JH)
Lenny Bruce — American (ND)
Let's Get Small (JMT)
Matching Tie and Handkerchief (MG)
Meet The Rutles (MS)
Monty Python: The Final Rip-Off (JO)
Monty Python's Previous Record (MG)
More of Tom Lehrer (MRe)
National Lampoon's Lemmings (JZ)
No Respect—Rodney Danger-

KEY (JB) Jeremy Banx; (RC) Roz Chast; (DC) David Chelsea; (ND) Nicholas Downes; (LF) Liana Finck; (TG) Tom Gammill; (RG) Rick Geary; (MG) Michael Gerber; (JG) Joey Green; (SG) Sam Gross; (JH) Jack Handey; (AJ) Al Jean; (TJ) Ted Jouflas; (AK) Adam Koford; (KK) Ken Krimstein; (DL) David Lancaster; (MM) Merrill Markoe; (BMc) Brian McConnachie; (PM) P.S. Mueller; (JO) Joe Oesterle; (MO) Mallory Ortberg; (BO) Ben Orlin; (DP) Dennis Perrin; (JP) Jonathan Plotkin; (MR) Mike Reddy; (MRe) Mike Reiss; (JR) Jay Ruttenberg; (LS) Lee Sachs; (KS) Katie Schwartz; (MS) Mark Simonson; (MSl) Michael Sloan; (NS) Nicholas Spooner; (RS) Rich Sparks; (BKT) B.K. Taylor; (JMT) Michael Thornton; (JAW) J.A. Weinstein; (MW) Michael Weithorn; (DV) Dirk Voetberg; (SY) Steve Young; (JZ) Jack Ziegler. **CARICATURES BY JOHN CUNEO.**

field (JAW)
Radio Dinner (MG)
Sail Away—Randy Newman (JMT)
That Nigger's Crazy (DP)
Schoolmates—Jim Copp and Ed Brown (RC)
The Smothers Brothers at the Purple Onion (JMT)
Stan Freberg Presents the United States of America, Volume One: The Early Years (PM)
Tom Lehrer (JMT)
The 2000-Year-Old Man (MM, JMT)
Weird Al in 3-D (AK, MR)
We're All Bozos on This Bus (JP)
Woody Allen: Standup Comic (JMT)

Movies
Airplane! (5x)
Animal Crackers (MO)
Animal House (NS)
Annie Hall (DP, JMT)
The Bad News Bears (JO)
Bananas (MRe)
Bedazzled (DC, MG)
Being John Malkovich (BO)
Billy Madison (JR)
Blazing Saddles (MO, JR, JMT)
The Boys in the Band (MO)
Bringing Up Baby (TJ)
Bullets Over Broadway (DL)
Caddyshack (JMT)
Cops by Buster Keaton (AJ)
City Lights (LF, AJ)
Dr. Strangelove (ND, MG, PM, DP, JMT)
Duck Soup (5x)
"Entirely a Matter for You"—Peter Cook (MG)
Galaxy Quest (MO, SY)
Ghostbusters (BO)

The Graduate (JO)
The Great Dictator (MRe)
The Great Muppet Caper (BO)
Groundhog Day (JMT)
A Hard Day's Night (MG)
Hollywood Shuffle (MO)
It's a Gift (RC)
The Jerk (AK, JO)
The Kid (JO)
Kingpin (MR)
The Lady Eve (AJ)
Life of Brian (MG, JMT, MS)
Little Big League (BO)
The Little Shop of Horrors (AK)

Midnight Run (BKT)
Mr. Hulot's Holiday (KK, MSI)
Monty Python and the Holy Grail (JH, JMT, DV, JAW)
Monty Python's The Meaning of Life (LS)
Modern Times (JO)
"Mollie Picon!" (Yiddish silent film actress) (LF)
Monkey Business (JR)
Mon Oncle (JB)
My Favorite Year (JO)
Network (BO)
A Night at the Opera (JG, LF, JO)
The Odd Couple (JO)
Office Space (RS, JMT)
One Week—Buster Keaton (MRe)
The Palm Beach Story (MRe)
The Party (MM)
The Princess Bride (BO, JMT)
The Producers (MG)
Radio Dinner (TJ)
Richard Pryor Live on the Sunset Strip (MG)
A Shot in the Dark (MG, JZ)
Sleeper (MRe)
Some Like It Hot (MG, AJ, MO)
Steamboat Bill, Jr. (JB)
Take the Money and Run (MW)

The 40-Year-Old Virgin (AJ)
There's Something About Mary (DV)
This Is Spinal Tap (JO, MS, JMT, DV)
Trading Places (MO)
Twentieth Century (MG)
Unfaithfully Yours (BMc)
"W.C. Fields — the full oeuvre" (MM)
Waiting for Guffman (BO)
When Harry Met Sally (BO, JMT)
Withnail and I (MM)
Young Frankenstein (MG, TG, JO, KS, JMT, DV)

Radio
Bob and Ray (6c)
The Goon Show (MG)
The Howard Stern Show (JO)
The Hitchhiker's Guide to the Galaxy (JAW)
Jean Shepherd (MG, BMc)
The National Lampoon Radio Hour (TG, DP, MS)
Tony Hancock (JB)

TV
"Albert Brooks's films in the first year of SNL" (MM)
All in the Family (JO, JP, MRe, KS, MSI)
All You Need Is Cash (MG, MS)
Blackadder (MG, JMT, DV)
Bill Hicks: Rant in E Minor (JMT)
A Bit of Fry and Laurie (MO)

Burns and Allen (MM)
Candid Camera (TG)
Cheers (BMc)
Dad's Army (JB)
The Dick Van Dyke Show (TG, TJ, MRe)
Eddie Izzard: Dress to Kill (MO, JMT)

Ernie Kovacs Show (PM)
Fawlty Towers (JMT, DV)
Frasier (BMc)
Freaks and Geeks (JMT)
Get Smart (TG, JG, MW)
Fridays (DP)
Home Improvement (BKT)
The Honeymooners (AJ)
Jack Benny (TG, MM)
Jeeves and Wooster (MG, JMT)
The Kids in the Hall (4x)
The Larry Sanders Show (JMT)
Late Night With David Letterman (JAW)
The League of Gentlemen (MO)

Looney Tunes (MG, JMT)
The Mary Tyler Moore Show (AJ)
Mitch Hedberg: Strategic Grill Locations (JMT)
Monty Python (10x)
Mr. Show (DP)
Mystery Science Theater 3000 (AK)
NewsRadio (MR, NS, JMT)
Not Only…But Also (MG, MO)
Police Squad (SY)
Ripping Yarns (MS)
Seinfeld (5x)
Sgt. Bilko (SG)
The Simpsons (MS)
SCTV (5x)
SNL (TG, DP)
Space Ghost Coast to Coast (RS)
The State (MO)

Moron, NOUN *(early 20th c. medical term):*
A person with a mental age of about 8 to 12.

*Fans of Hayes/Lois' **Esquire** will enjoy this parody, which was very nearly this issue's cover. But when Steve Brodner offers you art, you run it!*

A Beach Ball.

To Joey Green, it's a airplane pillow.

Gone are the days of complimentary in-flight champagne and cushy sleeping-car coaches on the Orient Express. Say hello to $50 "legroom upgrades" and bedbug-infested hotels. What's a weary traveler to do?

Hang tight—it's Joey Green to the rescue! ***Last-Minute Travel Secrets*** contains tons of ingenious travel tips that may sound quirky at first but really do work. You'll discover how to overcome obstacles using common household products, like how to . . .

- Sneak liquor aboard a cruise ship with food coloring
- Wash your clothes with a salad spinner
- Cook hot dogs in a coffee maker
- Seal hotel curtains with a clothes hanger
- And much, much more!

Last-Minute
TRAVEL
SECRETS
JOEY GREEN
121 INGENIOUS TIPS
TO ENDURE CRAMPED PLANES, CAR TROUBLE, AWFUL HOTELS, AND OTHER TRIPS FROM HELL

CHICAGO REVIEW PRESS

www.joeygreen.com

You can't make a website worth a damn.
But we can.
Contact us posthaste.
MerchantAndBlack.com

DELICIOUSLY SATISFYING CONTEMPORARY NOIR
a persuasive Hollywood thriller, taut and gutsy debut novel with clean, brilliant writing. *COLDWATER* by Diana Gould. In all formats, wherever books are sold. (Support your local independent bookstore.) Or, **http://amzn.to/2dJh1Kk**

THE KILLING TREE
Part funny. Part serious. Part cynical. All intelligent. J.D. Smith's fourth collection of poetry, from Finishing Line Press. Advance praise and ordering information available at: **http://bit.ly/2ebGJuw**

WRITING A BOOK? GETTING NOWHERE?
Don't give up – get help (from me!). I'm a ghostwriter/writing coach who partners with you one-on-one to get your book done. Packages range from 45-minute "Copy Therapy" sessions to twelve-week intensive book coaching programs. For more info, go to **copycoachlisa.com.**

CLOWN NOIR
James Finn Garner (*PC Bedtime Stories*) has a new mystery series for fans of noir, sideshow freaks and Americana. The "Rex Koko, Private Clown" thrillers have won Chicago Writers Association's Book of the Year TWICE! It's *Freaks* meets *The Maltese Falcon*. For info and samples, go to **rexkoko.com**, pally.

TABLETOP TALK - a YouTube channel for gamers by gamers. We create raw tabletop gaming content by filming our games. No scripts, just gaming. **www.youtube.com/user/TabletopTalk**

TOONS BY STEV-O (by Steve McGinn). some cartoons I hope'll make ya laff! drawn fresh in ink & then posted every day - 7 days a week! look for us on Facebook and The Comx Box Syndicate.

THE AMERICAN VALUES CLUB Crossword (formerly the Onion AV Club Crossword): It's rude, it's clued, and you'll get used to it.
Subscribe at avxword.com.

Buy **THE LAFAYETTE CAMPAIGN mybook.to/lafayettecampaign** "Andrew Updegrove brings a rare combination of drama, satire and technical accuracy to his writing. The result is a book you can't put down that tells you things you might wish you didn't know." - Admiral James G. Stavridis, former NATO Supreme Allied Commander Europe

THE VIRTUAL MEMORIES SHOW
What's the best books-art-comics-culture interview podcast you've never listened to? Discover The Virtual Memories Show at
www.chimeraobscura.com/vm/podcast-archive

I LOVE MAKING BEET CHIPS I love it so much that if you come to my apartment I will make some for you. I am not, to my knowledge, a serial killer. **@tinyrevolution.**

GEORGE BOOTH: cartoons, illustrations. Other services: grass fires stomped out and despots deterred. **929-210-0707**

HAVE WHAT IT TAKES TO BE A GOOBER DRIVER? Avoid World's Largest Peanuts envy. Navigate to offbeat tourist sights with the leaders for thirty years– **RoadsideAmerica.com.** Free e-subscription to Sightings. Easy sign-up. **RoadsideAmerica.com/newsletter**

SNOW ANGEL IS HERE!
In the tradition of The Tick and Venture Brothers comes this all-new hilarious full-color graphic novel about **SNOW ANGEL,** the newest tween superhero! From American Bystander contributor and Eisner nominee **DAVID CHELSEA**, this massive Dark Horse comic is fun for all ages (except, oddly, 37)! Available at your local bookstore, or email **dchelsea@comcast.com** to learn how you can receive a signed copy! GUARANTEED MERMAID FREE!

AN ILLUSTRATED ZARATHUSTRA
Hilarity ensues as excerpts and epigrams from Nietzsche's timeless classic comes to life in this madcap comic-strip-style dub version. Embrace your Fate and read it online at: **ScottMarshall.org**

BOOKS, POSTCARDS, ORIGINAL art by Rick Geary, available exclusively at **www.rickgeary.com**. I also take commissions.

FREE LUNCH!! NO BALONEY!
Attention all hungry cartoonists passing through Chicago: **Contact Jonathan Plotkin**
Editorial Cartoonist & Illustrator
Minister of Ways and Means
NCIS Chicago Chapter
Spontoonist@gmail.com
spontoonist.com

COMICS WITH PROBLEMS All problems solved. The Internet's BEST archive of the world's WEIRDEST comic books. **http://www.ep.tc/problems**

HACKER HUMOR You need tech humor, I've got it. Jokes, pitches, consulting, articles, posts. 35+ years experience (in parents' basement). ✉ **rob.warmowski@gmail.com**

YOUR ANDREW JACKSON $20s will soon be worthless! Use one to buy our non-award-winning, non-best-selling comedy anthology, **The Lowbrow Reader**, available from Drag City Books. Or check out the The Lowbrow Reader zine itself, eminently purchasable at **lowbrowreader.com.**

VEGETARIANS EATING HAGGIS PIZZA
Cosmic quarks! It's the Zen of Nimbus comic created by Michael Sloan. Nimbus, the celebrated immobile astronomer, is visited by a variety of repulsive creatures and events. Will they ever disturb his meditations? View the comic and blog, shop for Zen of Nimbus t-shirts and artwork:
www.zenofnimbus.com

EULOGIES WRITTEN ON DEMAND
Need a touching tribute...*stat*? Semi-professional eulogist offers her services. Quick turnaround guaranteed; encomium completed while the body's still warm or it's free. Little knowledge of the deceased in question necessary. Email **megan.koester@gmail.com** for rates.

WELCOME TO DISTRACTIONLAND
Too much time on your hands? Watch RANSACK RABBIT and other engaging animated entertainments. **Xeth Feinberg**, proprietor. As seen on the internet!
www.youtube.com/distractionland

UTILITY RIGHT FIELDER Available Also draws, writes. For more information contact Deerfield (Illinois) Little League. Or visit **kenkrimstein.com.**

UNICORN BOOTY WANTS YOU ...to read some of the most outrageously fun news, pop culture, and opinions on the web! Unicorn Booty serves up original news, film, TV, art, sports, fashion, travel and other weird wonders from around the world. Check us out at **http://unicornbooty.com.**

THE NEW YORK REVIEW OF SCIENCE FICTION
Reading Science Fiction Like It Matters for 28 Years. The first one's free! **http://www.nyrsf.com**

WANTED: MURDERER I'm looking for someone to kill me please, inquiries: **@ZackBornstein** on Twitter & Instagram

STRANGER THAN LIFE
250-page collection of single panel cartoons and strips from National Lampoon, The New Yorker, Playboy, Mother Jones and Arcade Comics by **MK Brown.** Available from Fantagraphics and Amazon. MK happy to inscribe. Contact at **mkbrown88@hotmail.com**

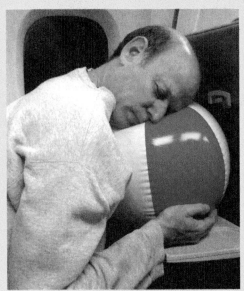

INDEX TO THIS ISSUE

Stuff you might not have noticed • By The Pleasure Syndicate

(continued) ☞

The Pleasure Syndicate *is Scott Jacobson, Todd Levin, Mike Sacks and Ted Travelstead.*

NICK SPOONER

"Of course I find you attractive. I just prefer it with the lights off."

KUPER

"Stop calling me 'a Cassandra.' You don't know any other Cassandras!"

☞ (*CRUISIN' continued from p. 38*)

you will find the severed head of the screenwriter, his eyelids nibbled away by Mickey before each showing, only to grow back again. Trivia: Can you name that screenwriter? No, you can't, because he's been forgotten.

REMINDER

Remember that red-eye from LAX to JFK where you had six vodka cranberries and then you screamed at that attendant for saying "Please remember" all the goddamn time? Please remember that.

GLUTTON ALERT!

Don't forget (please remember) to join Captain Pluto for our Midnight Snack. Chef Ratatouille and his all-rodent kitchen have scurried up an infectious feast.

Enjoy Farmer Donald's Ducky Guacamole with Chip and Dale, Nemo Niçoise, Chopped Chicken Little salad, Geppetto's Wood-Fired Pizza, gluten-free pasta with your choice of Toad Fra Diavolo or Baloognese sauce, Thumper Hasenpfeffer, Lion King Pao, Mushu (Tastes Like) Chicken, Poached Dory stuffed with Sebastian Florentine, Roast Beast au jus de Belle, Braised Shank of Bambi's mom with a glaze of human tears, and for dessert, Deep-fried Cinnamon Dumbo Ears or Queen Grimhilde's Wicked Apple Popovers with your choice of creme Grumpé or salted salt ice cream.

Eat until you're about to burst, and then continue eating. Also, please remember there is a three-drink minimum from Eeyore's Champagne Fountain of Regret. Check with Princess Elsa to see if you have been chosen to be an ice sculpture.

This is your cruise director Larry signing off and saying how very, very sorry he is, so so sorry, he had no idea when he stiffed that cruise director, that that would — I mean, it was all-inclusive — and she was so goddamn perky all the time, and — *Ayeee! What the hell, this isn't my rending time!* — but I'm just saying, I've, I've repented and I'm sorry and *please —*
  Good Morning!   **B**

BY MATT MATERA & ALAN GOLDBERG

THE SIMPSONS DID IT

Spoilers on page 92

ACROSS

1. Play things
6. Start to meet?
10. Most-watched TV finale (a record even *The Simpsons* is unlikely to beat)
14. Bizarre
15. Shawarma holder
16. Pilot's beginning, at times
17. Phlegmatic like an ancient Greek
18. "Write a wise saying and your name will live forever" source, for short
19. If you smelt it, you may have dealt it
20. Rip-off of "Marge vs. the Monorail" (classic quote: "A town with money is like a mule with a spinning wheel.")
23. Overnight option more sheltered than an outt?
24. Not upright
25. MacArthur genius grant winner and writer of the "Black Panther" comic
27. Brees or Newton
30. Therefore, a logical choice
31. What no one goes to Moe's to do
32. Knockoff of "Homer at the Bat" (classic quote: "Hypnotist: You will give 110%. Team: That's impossible no one can give more than 100%. By definition that's the most anyone can give.")
38. Faulty concealment for Polonius
41. The loneliest number (*N.B.*: numbers probably don't feel emotion)
42. Ethiopian leader Selassie
43. Pale imitation of "Bart of Darkness" (classic quote: "Shut up, brain! I've got friends. I don't need you anymore.")
46. Actor Hagen who taught Liza Minnelli and Al Pacino
47. Slowly lessen
48. Los ___ (Manhattan Project hub)
51. Capital of Tasmania
53. Truck fare?
55. "Let's kick some ___" (horrible Mr. Freeze pun from *Batman and Robin*)
56. Tired retread of "Simpsoncalifragilisticexpiala-D'ohcious" (classic quote: "The nanny we want is kindly and sage / And one who will work for minimum wage.")
61. Hairstyle popular in the '80s
63. Potter's oven
64. Channing Tatum or Bettie Page
65. Prefix with –normal or –Norman
66. Fencing sword
67. Actor Christensen of *Traffic* (and Hallmark movie *My Boyfriends' Dogs*)
68. Dark-colored mineral
69. 6-8 in Milan
70. Dissuade

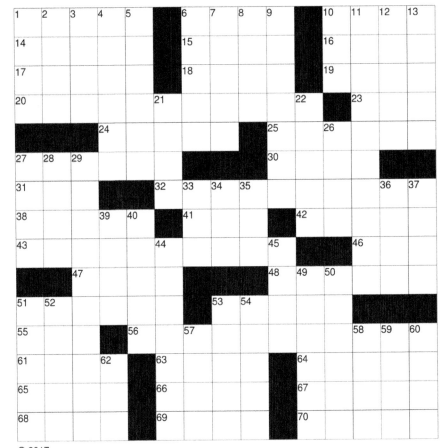

© 2017

DOWN

1. What to read on Saturday evening?
2. Subject of Boston's biggest blunder?
3. First American Indian tribe met by Lewis and Clark
4. Prepares for a night on the town
5. Triple-deadbolted
6. Nation with rain on plains
7. Frequent pun response
8. One of about ten quadrillion vigintillion in the universe
9. Silver bullet (well, if werewolves truly represent all your problems)
10. Best-selling Chinese author
11. Principal place of assembly?
12. Great on stage, lousy in your kidneys
13. Bugles
21. Ilk
22. *Dinosaur Comics* author Ryan
26. Rio, por ejemplo
27. Stilton partner
28. Longest river entirely in Switzerland
29. Former Met all-star outfielder who cries in "Homer at the Bat"
33. Pet name

34. *The* _____ (final book in Lemony Snicket series)
35. Protagonist in *The Matrix Revolutions*
36. Type of saxophone
37. Meadows (not Tim or Audrey)
39. Sector 7-G, e.g.
40. "No, s'not too cold for bees"?
44. Admissions statistic
45. Birthplace of Steve Martin
49. Cut
50. Dream
51. African river dweller that may be hungry, hungry
52. "Blonde" singer Frank
53. Late comedic genius Mary _____ Moore
54. Sleep disorder fixed by continuous positive air pressure device
57. What 19-across can be
58. Still alive
59. Zap in the microwave
60. Engage in a war of words
62. *Rushmore* main character Fischer **B**

CPSIA information can be obtained
at www.ICGtesting.com
Printed in the USA
LVOW05s2216050517
533454LV00006B/8/P